What Counts as a
Good Job in Teaching?

What Counts as a Good Job in Teaching?

Becoming a Teacher as We Race to the Top

Colleen Gilrane and Kristin Rearden

ROWMAN & LITTLEFIELD
Lanham • Boulder • New York • London

Published by Rowman & Littlefield
A wholly owned subsidiary of The Rowman & Littlefield Publishing Group, Inc.
4501 Forbes Boulevard, Suite 200, Lanham, Maryland 20706
www.rowman.com

Unit A, Whitacre Mews, 26-34 Stannery Street, London SE11 4AB, United Kingdom

Copyright © 2015 by Rowman & Littlefield Publishers, Inc.

British Library Cataloguing in Publication Information Available

Library of Congress Cataloging-in-Publication Data

ISBN 978-1-4422-3469-7 (cloth : alk. paper) ISBN 978-1-4422-3470-3 (pbk. : alk.
paper) — ISBN 978-1-4422-3471-0 (electronic)

∞™ The paper used in this publication meets the minimum requirements of
American National Standard for Information Sciences—Permanence of Paper
for Printed Library Materials, ANSI/NISO Z39.48-1992.

Printed in the United States of America

Contents

Prelude: The Chaotic State of Teacher Evaluation in the
          United States   xi
       Situating Preservice Teacher Education in the Chaos   xiii

PART I: THE UNDERGRADUATE PREINTERNSHIP MINOR
Colleen P. Gilrane

1 Overview   3
   The Spring Block: Practicum and Teaching Methods   4
   Planning the New and Improved Spring Block   6
      Getting Feedback and Fine-Tuning   8
      Did the Four Essential Questions Fit the Rubrics?   9
      Course Design   11
   Implementing the Plan   12
      Course Organization   13
         Models of Effective Teaching (2 weeks)   14
         Who Are My Students? What Do I Want Them to Learn?
           (2 weeks)   19
         Assessment: What Would Count as a Good Job? (2 weeks) 19
         What Resources Are Available to Me? How Do I Organize
           Them to Support Learning? (3 weeks)   19
         Designing Your Learning Plans (5 weeks of Workshop
           Time)   19
      Final Evaluation Conferences   23

2 Question #1: Who Are My Students?   24
Who Are My Students: Candidates as Colleen's Kids   25
  The Dear Colleen Letter   25
  What Do My Candidates Care About?   27
  What Kinds of Help Do My Candidates Need?   28
    Classroom/Course Structures   28
    Specific Strategies   28
    Responses My Candidates Need from Me   29
  How Do My Candidates Want/Need to Be Assessed? To
    Be Taught?   30
Who Are My Students: Candidates Watching *Their* Kids   31
  Addressing Diversity in Our Friday Classes   31
    Conferences Addressing Diversity during Workshop Time   31
    Class Session Addressing Diversity as a Stand-Alone Topic   32
Who Are My Students: What Did Candidates Learn?   35

3 Question #2: What Do I Want Them to Learn?   37
Specific Supports for Thinking about Content   38
  Class Session Addressing Content as a Stand-Alone Topic   38
  The Understanding by Design Framework   41
What Do I Want Them to Learn: What Did Candidates Learn?   42
  Connecting Students to Content   42
  The Process of Identifying Content Worth Learning   43
  The Importance of Depth over Coverage   44

4 Question #3: What Would Count as Evidence of Learning?   45
Learning about Assessment by Being Assessed   46
  Formative Assessment of My Candidates   46
  Summative Assessment of My Candidates   47
    Grades for the Friday Portion of ELED 422   48
Friday Class Sessions Devoted to Assessment as a Stand-
  Alone Topic   50
  Performance Assessment   50
  Formative Assessment   52
Designing Assessments for Learning Plans   53
What Would Count as Evidence: What Did Candidates Learn?   54
  Assessment Beyond Worksheets and Tests   54
  Bringing a Critical Lens to Current Practice   55
  Bringing Student Experiences to Bear on Designing
    Assessments as Teachers   56

5 Question #4: How Do I Get There?   57
Selecting Instructional Materials   57
Selecting Personnel Resources and Instructional Strategies   59

Making Decisions about Time, Space, Environment, and Pulling
  It All Together   63
How Do I Get There: What Did Candidates Learn?   63
  Expanded Awareness of Resources   64
  Time as a Resource   65
  Personnel as Resources   65

INTERLUDE: VOICES OF CANDIDATES

6 Hannah's Reflection   69
   Hannah Louderback
   Transitioning to Internship   70
   First-Year Teaching after Internship   71
     Teaching Science: Erosion Unit   72
     Teaching Math: Problems with Missing or Extra Information   73
   Final Reflections   74

7 Jessica's Reflection   76
   Jessica Covington
   "Understanding" Across Differing Teaching Contexts   76
     Using Knowledge of Students to Set Goals and
       Evaluate Learning   77
       Setting Learning Goals   78
       Evaluating Learning   79
   What Worked for Me: The W.H.E.R.E.T.O. Strategy   80
     Where   80
     Hook   81
     Equip   81
     Rethink and Revise   81
     Self-Evaluation   82
     Tailor   82
     Organize   82
   Final Reflections   82

PART II: THE GRADUATE INTERNSHIP YEAR
   Kristin T. Rearden

8 Getting Started: Orienting and Building Relationships   87
   Preparing for the Field Experience: Setting up the Seminar Class 88
     Physical Design of the Seminar Classroom   88
     The Opening Class Session   89
     Preparing to Enter the Schools: First Impressions   89
   The Field Experience   90
     The Spectrum of Classroom Environments   91

Focal Point One: School Culture   92
Focal Point Two: The Classroom Environment   94
Focal Point Three: The Planning Process   95
Focal Point Four: Instructional Strategies   98
Focal Point Five: Assessment Strategies   100
Final Reflections   101

9 Fall Semester: Overlaying Good Teaching with Team Rubrics   103
Initial Weeks of the Internship   103
    Physical Space Considerations   103
    Establishing a Presence   105
    Assuming Responsibility for Planning, Teaching,
        and Assessing   108
Developing Planning Skills   110
    Lesson Plans: Novice and Veteran Approaches   110
    Questions: At the Heart of Learning to Plan   112
Preparing for Formal Evaluations   115
    The "Dry Run" Evaluation   116
        The Lesson Plan: Intended versus Implemented   117
        Areas to Improve and Areas of Strength   117
        Assessment Data   119
        Analyzing the Lesson with Evaluation Rubrics   119
The Initial Evaluation for State Licensure   121

10 Spring Semester: Overlaying Good Teaching with edTPA Rubrics   124
Growing into Their Roles as Teachers   124
    Leading, Not Soloing   125
    Viewing Themselves as Teachers   126
    Recognizing Beliefs about the Importance of Education   128
Theory into Practice: Action Research and Problem-
    Based Research Review   129
Blending the edTPA into Our Teacher Preparation Program   131
    Supporting the Interns during the edTPA Process   131
    Changes to the Program   134
    Evidence of Success   136

Coda: The Importance of an Inquiry-Based, Workshop Approach   138
How Did Candidates Respond?   140
    TEAM Results   140
    edTPA Results   141
    Task 1 Planning   141
    Task 2 Instruction   142

    Task 3 Assessment   142
    edTPA Total Score and Cutoff   144
   Candidates' Reflections   145
  Discussion   147

Bibliography   149

Index   155

About the Authors   163

Prelude: The Chaotic State of Teacher Evaluation in the United States

In 2011, attention paid to teacher evaluation in the United States in general, and in our state of Tennessee in particular, intensified in response to the Race to the Top program (McGuinn, 2012). The American Educational Research Association (AERA) and the National Academy of Education convened the Capitol Hill research briefing in September 2011 "as part of these organizations' commitment to the sound use of scientific research and data in education and education policy" (Darling-Hammond, Amrein-Beardsley, Haertel, & Rothstein, 2011, p. i). A background paper prepared for policymakers opened as follows:

> There is a widespread consensus among practitioners, researchers, and policy makers that current teacher evaluation systems in most school districts do little to help teachers improve or to support professional decision making. For this reason, new approaches to teacher evaluation are being developed and tested. (Darling-Hammond et al., 2011, p. 1)

In that initial year, much was said about this issue (Wilson, Rozelle, & Mikeska, 2011), but the coherence of the discussion was much less clear (Wiseman, 2012). There were multiple sets of guidelines for the design of teacher evaluation systems (Curtis & Wiener, 2012; Darling-Hammond et al., 2011; Goe, Holdheide, & Miller, 2011; Wilson et al., 2011) and for the evaluation of those designed (Glazerman et al., 2012; Shakman et al., 2012). Advice was available to support those who wished to include value-added assessments as part of an overall system (Glazerman et al., 2012), as well as advice that value-added models are unstable and are affected by student differences (Darling-Hammond et al., 2011). All of the negative effects of high-stakes assessments that we had lamented for years with respect to the learning of P–12 students (McCarthey, 2008; Perelman, 2008; Taylor, 2008) had become a reality for the learning of our teachers.

As we write in spring 2014, the situation is no more coherent even as it has grown more intense, both in practice and in the literature. Among those who endorse the use of value-added growth models, there continues to be disagreement about which models to use (Ehlert, Koedel, Parsons, & Podgursky, 2012). Meanwhile, there are voices continuing to advise against the use of value-added models based on test scores (Darling-Hammond, 2013; Mathis, 2012) and calling for the use of more high-quality student growth data (Darling-Hammond, 2013; Goe, Biggers, & Croft, 2012) and suggesting that "in order to be most useful, evidence of student learning should be directly connected to specific content as well as to delivery of that content (i.e., instructional practices) (Goe et al., 2012, p. 9). On April 8, 2014, the American Statistical Association released its *ASA Statement on Using Value-Added Models for Educational Assessment*, intended to "provide guidance, given current knowledge and experience, as to what can and cannot reasonably be expected from the use of VAMs," and included these in a list of limitations:

- VAMs are generally based on standardized test scores, and do not directly measure potential teacher contributions toward other student outcomes.
- VAMs typically measure correlation, not causation: effects—positive or negative—attributed to a teacher may actually be caused by other factors that are not captured in the model. (American Statistical Association, 2014, p. 2)

Think tanks and research centers at every position on the political spectrum are expressing concern about the speed with which decisions are being made and implemented, and suggesting caution about using the results of these new high-stakes evaluations before they are thoroughly tested. The Center for American Progress (McGuinn, 2012), the National Education Policy Center (Mathis, 2012), the National Center for the Analysis of Longitudinal Data in Education Research (Ehlert et al., 2012), and the National Comprehensive Center for Teacher Quality (Goe et al., 2012) have all published reports, and in September 2012 the American Enterprise Institute for Public Policy Research characterized the situation as follows:

Yet the recent evaluation binge is not without risks. By nature, education policymaking tends to lurch from inattention to overreach. When a political moment appears, policymakers and advocates rush to take advantage as quickly as they can, knowing that opportunities for real change are fleeting. This is understandable, and arguably necessary, given the nature of America's political system. But headlong rushes inevitably produce unintended consequences—something akin to a policy hangover as ideas move from conception to implementation. (Mead, Rotherham, & Brown, 2012, p. 3)

This statement now seems almost prescient with respect to a January 2013 policy analysis that had this to say about the use of value-added growth models as part of a teacher's evaluation:

Due process is violated where administrators or other decision-makers place blind faith in the quantitative measures, assuming them to be causal and valid (attributable to the teacher) and applying arbitrary and capricious cutoff points to those measures (performance categories leading to dismissal). The problem, as we see it, is that some of these new state statutes require these due process violations, even where the informed, thoughtful professional understands full well that she is being forced to make a wrong decision. They require that decision makers take action based on these measures even against their own informed professional judgment. (Baker, Oluwole, & Green, 2013, p. 19)

SITUATING PRESERVICE TEACHER EDUCATION IN THE CHAOS

Despite the myriad and often conflicting perspectives among scholars and practitioners about what should count as evidence of effective teaching, some states (including ours) have reified high-stakes teacher evaluation by increasing the frequency and intensity of the assessments themselves (including greater sanctions attached to value-added data) and tying them to issues of salary, promotion, and tenure. Teachers and administrators are alienated and exhausted, teacher educators and scholars are frustrated and angry, and our teacher candidates are trying to figure out how to navigate the constantly shifting landscape.

As overwhelming as all of this is for teachers and administrators, try to imagine how much more so it must be for teacher candidates—who might even be wondering if they ought to enter the profession in the first place—and for their faculty instructors and mentors who are tasked with preparing them to be successful when "success" is a more frenetic moving target than it has ever been. Preservice teachers at our institution carry out a full-year graduate internship during which they are evaluated by the same system as teachers in the district in which they are teaching, so that any changes in our state evaluation system have an immediate impact on our candidates.

As one of the first Race to the Top winners (McGuinn, 2012), Tennessee completely changed its teacher evaluation system in the summer of 2011. Our interns and their faculty supervisors learned "on the go" how to teach and supervise using new rubrics alongside the teachers and principals with whom they work in local schools. Our cohort of interns teaches in a system that uses the statewide Tennessee Educator Acceleration Model (TEAM); this educator rubric used to collect observation data (for 50 percent of the evaluation) includes sections on Instruction, Planning, and Environment (see http://team-tn.org/assets/educator-resources/TEAM_Educator_Rubric.pdf). Student growth as measured by the Tennessee Value-Added Assessment System (TVAAS) accounts for 35 percent of a total evaluation, with the remaining 15 percent consisting of "student achievement data selected by the educator and his/her supervisor from a list of state board approved options" (McGuinn, 2012, p. 12).

In addition, our institution has participated since the initial field testing in the Teacher Performance Assessment Consortium (TPAC) (Darling-Hammond, 2006a; Hill, Hansen, & Stumbo, 2011). Our state has allowed candidates who are successful to use their edTPA score in lieu of the Principles of Learning and Teaching Praxis exam required for licensure. edTPA includes rubrics for Planning, Instruction, Assessment, Analyzing Teaching Effectiveness, and Academic Language. Our candidates are evaluated according to edTPA during the same internship year as they are evaluated according to TEAM.

During the 2010/2011 academic year, elementary education faculty were in the process of redesigning a preinternship block hoping to better meet the needs of our prospective teachers, to align with changes that were already planned for the internship year itself. The statewide changes described above were implemented in summer 2011, thus serving as a prelude to our first offering of the "new" spring block in spring 2012, to candidates whom we now knew would be evaluated the following year according to both TEAM and edTPA rubrics. Included in conversations among various faculty groups as we planned were these questions: Should we organize around the edTPA rubrics? Should we organize around the TEAM rubrics? What if the state and/or district changes again in two or three years? What if our interns get jobs in other states or districts?

Keeping in mind that a teacher's career may last for as many as thirty-five years, we believe the need is greater than ever for educator preparation that supports teachers in whatever situations they may find themselves, with whatever evaluation schemes may be used to judge their work. We want to help prospective teachers develop the habits of mind (Eisner, 2002) that support teaching for deep understanding even as their lived experiences as novice teachers conspire to encourage them to "study for the test" of the next day's evaluation rubric. We focus our efforts on helping our candidates learn

1. to plan and teach for deep understanding, then
2. to document the important things they are doing, and finally

3. to articulate those important things according to the terminology of which-
   ever evaluation scheme or rubric is in play in the situation.

In this book, we share our efforts at offering such a preparation, and its
impact on two cohorts of candidates. In Part I, Colleen Gilrane takes the lead
in describing our undergraduate elementary minor, with particular emphasis
on the spring block of courses our candidates take immediately preceding
their internship year. Chapter 1 provides an overview, and outlines the process through which we arrived at the self-monitoring questions that form the
basis of the enduring understandings (Wiggins & McTighe, 2005) we hope
our candidates will take into their careers, and onto which we believe any
sound set of teacher evaluation standards can be mapped. Chapters 2 through
5 each focuses on one of these: Who are my students? What do I want them
to learn? What would count as evidence of learning? and How do I get there?
Each chapter includes scholarship supporting that habit of mind (Eisner,
2002), descriptions and examples of instructional strategies and candidates'
work samples, and reflections by the candidates themselves, both before and
after engaging in the course experiences.

In the Interlude, we take time to listen more deeply to two students' voices.
Chapter 6 is Hannah Louderback's reflection on our model and how it played
out in her internship year and then in her first year as a paid teacher. Hannah
was an elementary preintern in 2011/2012, interned during the 2012/2013
school year, and taught fourth-grade in a public school during 2013/2014.
Jessica Covington reflects from a slightly different perspective in chapter 7.
As a special education major, she participated in the spring block as a junior,
and then spent 2012/2013 completing 280 hours of practicum in special
education (140 hours each in modified and comprehensive settings). She
completed her internship during 2013/2014.

Kristin Rearden takes the lead in Part II, which focuses on the graduate
internship year. In chapter 8, she describes how to get the year off to a good
start, beginning during the spring block when she facilitates their practicum
experiences. Chapter 9 focuses on the fall semester when interns design and
carry out a learning segment focused on good teaching for deep understanding, and are evaluated according to the Planning and Instruction rubrics of
the TEAM evaluation system. In chapter 10, we see how students take that
or another learning segment (which was video recorded) and reflect on it according to the edTPA system.

Finally, in the Coda, we reflect on the importance of an inquiry-based,
workshop approach in our work with teachers.

Part I

THE UNDERGRADUATE PREINTERNSHIP MINOR

Colleen P. Gilrane

Chapter One

Overview

Candidates for elementary education licensure at the University of Tennessee, Knoxville, complete undergraduate degrees in arts and sciences majors, as well as an elementary education minor. Many of the courses in the minor are "restricted" in enrollment, and candidates may not take them until they have been through a rigorous admissions process that includes review of transcripts and test scores, speech and hearing screening, written application, background check, and interview by a four-person Admissions Board composed of program faculty, arts and sciences faculty, teachers and administrators from partnership schools, and current candidates. As graduate students, they carry out a full-year internship for which they receive one year of credit on salary schedules and pension schedules in Tennessee. In addition to the internship itself, as graduate students they must complete two additional methods courses, and receive passing scores on edTPA and the Praxis exams required by our state to receive their licenses. The program is organized as shown in table 1.1.

There are eight courses, for a total of twenty-five semester hours, in the undergraduate minor. Four of the classes may be taken at any time that they fit a candidate's schedule, with the additional caveat that one must be formally admitted to teacher education to take the reading class and the technology class. The remaining components, a blend of coursework and practicum, are to be taken concurrently in the spring semester immediately preceding their full-year internship. The Ed Psych and Special Ed courses are offered at a variety of times to support the challenges our candidates face in scheduling, especially those who still have courses to finish in their academic majors, and candidates are free to enroll in the sections that best fit their schedules. The elementary education courses are referred to as the senior spring block, and

Table 1.1.   Elementary Licensure Program

Undergraduate		*Graduate Professional Year*	
Arts & Sciences baccalaureate major	*Elementary Education minor*	*Fall*	*Spring*
	Ed Psych 210 *Human Development* Info Sciences 330 *Children's Literature* Ed Tech 486 *Instructional Computing* Reading Ed 430 *Elem Reading* Spring Block • Ed Psych 401 *Applied Ed Psych* • Special Ed 402 *Diverse Learners* • Elem Ed 351 *Practicum* • Elem Ed 422 *Integrated Methods*	• Professional Internship Teaching *4 days per week* • Graduate methods course Reading, Math, Science, or Social Studies *(Friday a.m.)* • Analysis of Teaching for Professional Development *(Friday p.m.)*	• Professional Internship Teaching *4 days per week* • Graduate methods course Reading, Math, Science, or Social Studies *(Friday a.m.)* • Clinical Studies *(Friday p.m.)*
		• 2 Add'l Graduate Methods Courses • Satisfactory Praxis and/or edTPA	

candidates experience them as cohorts who spend the spring and then their internship year together in the same schools with the same university mentors. In our case, I (Colleen) was instructor of record for our cohort's Elementary Education 422 course, and Kristin for the Elementary Education 351 and the graduate internship.

THE SPRING BLOCK:
PRACTICUM AND TEACHING METHODS

As we mentioned in the introduction, we implemented a redesigned block in the spring of 2012. The new design was intended to improve aspects of the block that both we and our candidates had identified as needing attention.

For the two elementary education courses, we blocked out four hours each on Monday, Wednesday, and Friday mornings, and organized that time as shown in table 1.2. Our candidates rotated among three different instructors for five-week introductions to science, social studies, and mathematics teaching on Monday mornings, and spent Wednesday mornings in field experiences that Kristin describes thoroughly in chapter 8. My assignment was to design the Friday segment to support our candidates in pulling together their field experiences and coursework to date, and figuring out what to do with it!

While I had been working with candidates for years as an instructor of the Reading Education 430 course, and seeing many of them again in a graduate literacy course, I had not formally taught the spring block in a long time. Fortunately, those of us who would be organizing the Friday segments had several meetings over the summer and fall of 2011, leading up to our first implementation in spring 2012. Remember that this was the same summer of 2011 that our state introduced the brand new Tennessee Educator Acceleration Model (TEAM); our candidates would be evaluated with it during their internship year, so being sure that they were prepared was part of our conversation. And keep in mind, our candidates were already required to complete edTPA (Darling-Hammond, 2006a; Stanford Center for Assessment Learning and Equity, 2013) during their internship year, as we had been involved with it since the pilot stage.

We had much thoughtful conversation about these rubrics, the relative merits of them, and the long-term value they might have for our candidates. TEAM was in place in most of the districts in which they might eventually

Table 1.2. The Elementary Senior Spring Block

Monday: Content	Wednesday: Field experience	Friday: Pulling it all together
• introduction to Science Education *(5 weeks)*	• K–2 placement (6 weeks)	Colleen's class designing learning plans:
• introduction to Social Studies education *(5 weeks)*	• visits to internship schools (1 week)	1. Who are my students?
• introduction to Math Education *(5 weeks)*	• 3–5 placement (6 weeks)	2. What do I want them to learn?
	• mix of rural, urban, suburban placements	3. What will count as a good job?
	• meet with Kristin weekly for reflection	4. How will I get there?

work in Tennessee, but not all . . . and the summer of 2011 showed us how quickly that could change. Among the districts where we place interns were some of those in the state selecting another approved system. And of course edTPA, as valuable as it is, has no longevity beyond the internship year.

I can still remember how I felt when I finally sat down and looked at these rubrics. TEAM has three different rubrics on which there are indicators for Significantly Above Expectations (5), At Expectations (3), and Significantly Below Expectations (1); scores of 4 and 2 may be assigned. The Instruction rubric has twelve items that include fifty-seven sets of indicators, the Planning rubric has three items that include thirteen sets of indicators, and the Environment rubric has four items that include eighteen sets of indicators. But that's not all! The version of edTPA that was in use while we were planning our new block included rubrics for three general questions each in the areas of Planning, Instruction, Assessment, and Academic Language; in all, twenty-seven different items.

Take a minute to think about that. Nineteen items across three rubrics, scored using eighty-eight different indicators, for TEAM. Twelve items across four rubrics, scored using twenty-seven different indicators, for edTPA. I remember being stunned by this and thinking, "We have lost our minds!" And wondering how to bring coherence to this situation for our candidates, who were nervous listening to the frustration of teachers as TEAM rolled out across our state.

PLANNING THE NEW AND IMPROVED SPRING BLOCK

I spent a good amount of time reflecting back on thirty-four years (at that time) of being a professional educator whose career had spanned many iterations of standards, rubrics, and management systems. I knew that—trite as it sounds—I believed that *good teaching is good teaching*, even as it differs at various levels (I've taught from first grade through advanced graduate programs) and in various disciplines. *That very differentiation* is one of the things that makes it good teaching! What were those core things that I attended to, that made my teaching successful across different settings that were not even all at schools? If I could articulate those, perhaps they could help make these rubrics seem less overwhelming. My first draft was simple: Who are my students? What do I want them to learn? What would count as a good job? And how do I get there once I know these things?

I can never begin teaching without asking myself, *who are my students?* I cannot fathom planning and teaching without this knowledge; in fact, when I was in graduate school and teaching undergraduates, the hardest part for me was figuring out how to teach methods courses without children! I'd just spent four years in a district office in a position called Resource Teacher/ Trainer, and my job was to work alongside teachers in their classrooms as they worked to improve their literacy instruction. I knew them, and I knew their children. How else can you teach? Or teach someone how to teach?

I am aware that there are people who believe that following a script or adhering to a teachers' manual is teaching. I am not one of them; in fact, my colleague Amy Broemmel and I have been fairly insistent over the years that our Reading Education 430 students do *not* write lesson plans, as they are not in field experience placements while taking the class. We do not wish to support the idea that teaching is performing! But in ELED 422, there would be real children in the field experience placements, and asking candidates to plan with these children in mind made sense. Surely helping them learn to think deeply about children from different perspectives would support their being successful according to these rubrics?

Another critical question I ask myself is *what do I want them to learn?* And this means so much more than standards or curriculum frameworks. What's important? What's the essence? This is tied intimately to my third question, *what would count as a good job of learning?* What is it we want learners to do with their learning? Too much of schooling just asks for knowledge to be displayed on worksheets, or recognized on multiple-choice tests, or written in some rote fashion (such as a three- or five-paragraph essay). I find Wittgenstein's (1953) idea of knowledge-in-use to be very helpful here, as thinking about what learners need to do with their knowledge shapes that very knowledge itself. Authenticity is important to me, and I like to think about the way knowledge and skills are used in real life and try to bring that into my classroom, rather than settling for academic exercises.

Finally, having thought about all of these things, I can ask myself, *how am I going to get there?* What materials, time, and personnel resources might I use? How might I organize them? Which materials might I *not* use, even if provided for free by the district or publisher, because they do not help me accomplish what I've decided is important? It is amazing how simple the decisions about what's worth my time—and what's not—become once I've thought through the previous questions.

Having articulated these, which I have come to call "essential questions," borrowing the language of the Understanding by Design framework (McTighe & Thomas, 2003; Wiggins & McTighe, 2005), I had to think about how to enact them in ELED 422 itself. My students would be preservice teachers, preparing to carry out a full-year internship after the spring block. They would have had an introductory reading course already and would be getting introduced to science, social studies, and math by content specialists

concurrent to my working with them; they'd also be carrying out two different field experiences. If my job was to help them begin to think about pulling
this together, I needed to ask, *what do real teachers do*, once they know their
students, and their content, and what outcomes they are working toward?
They *plan and teach*. They don't take tests, they don't write reflections—they
plan and teach. Our final products would be learning plans.

Getting Feedback and Fine-Tuning

Throughout the fall of 2011, I hounded students, friends, and colleagues
for feedback on my framework and plans. My fall courses were a section
of the Reading Education 430 course as well as a graduate literacy course.
The students in the reading education course, as prospective 422 students,
were highly invested and glad to know they did not need to panic about the
rubrics—or, at least, to know that *I believed* they did not need to panic! I was
able to receive feedback from many different teachers: the students in my
graduate class, the members of my teacher research group, and some teachers
in a school that was a research site. They liked the plan but pushed more on
the framework, with their own experiences sometimes making them wonder
if I'd left out something important. This was a crucial conversation for me,
as with over three decades of teaching experience, so many of these things
had become second nature to me that I did not give them conscious attention;
indeed, Noel Burch's (Adams, 2011) term *unconsciously competent* might fit!
I needed to make my thinking public (Paris & Winograd, 2003), and these
conversations helped flesh out the details. Eventually, the four essential questions and their subparts looked like this.

1. Who are my students?
   - What do they know?
   - What do they care about?
   - What can they do?
   - What kind of help do they need?
2. What do I want them to learn?
   - really big ideas worth learning
   - this includes, but is not limited to, standards
   - this includes, but is not limited to, academic language
3. What would count as a good job? (assessment)
   - authentic application
   - ongoing feedback/coaching
   - real-life scenarios requiring synthesis, critical thinking

4. How will I get there? (marshal resources to accomplish #2 and #3?)
  - materials
  - time
  - personnel
  - environment
  - space
  - routines
  - activities/strategies/engagements
  - teaching roles

The final product was also discussed and fleshed out, not only in these conversations but also with Kristin and those who would be teaching the other cohorts, as we talked about ways to have an authentic product that would support excellent teaching and that also looked ahead to the real world of TEAM and edTPA in our interns' lives. Since it is important for candidates to think about learning over time rather than isolated lessons, and edTPA required a three-to-five-day learning segment for analysis, the requirement for ELED 422 would be a learning plan covering at least three to five days, in a content area and grade level of the candidates' choice, aligned with the *Understanding by Design* design standards (McTighe & Wiggins, 2004, p. 24), which are described in chapter 5. As the district in which our candidates would be interning had its own required TEAM lesson plan form, our candidates would also take one day of their learning plan and map it out in detail using that form, then self-assess according to the TEAM planning rubric. Our hope was for them to see that by thinking carefully about the essential questions, and planning for their students' deep understanding of content, they would be in fine shape with respect to the rubrics.

Did the Four Essential Questions Fit the Rubrics?

I knew that if this hope were to stand any chance of being realized, the candidates needed to have confidence that there was, indeed, sufficient overlap among the four questions, TEAM, and edTPA. I approached this as a sorting exercise with manipulatives: My four questions printed on bright blue paper as category headers, the TEAM rubric items listed on a yellow legal pad and cut apart, and the edTPA rubric items listed on a white legal pad and cut apart. I set up a card table in the sewing room down the hall from my study at home, arranged the four headers, and went to work. The results, glued to a poster board so that I could share them with the candidates, are shown in figure 1.1.

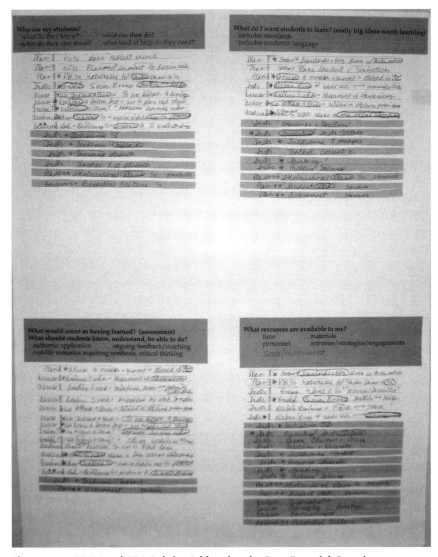

Figure 1.1.   TEAM and TPA Rubrics Addressing the Four Essential Questions

I had made several photocopies of the rubric items before beginning—in case I made mistakes—and was soon glad I had for another reason. Quite a few of the items from each of the two sets of rubrics needed to be sorted into more than one of my essential questions, so I needed two or three copies of those items, which I color-coded with magic markers to show that they were the same rubric item. It took quite a while, as I consulted the complete rubrics to be sure I was keeping all of the indicators for each item in mind as I placed it, but in the end, all of the TEAM and edTPA rubric items were subsumed under the four essential questions. I could, with confidence, ask candidates to trust the plan, focus on planning and teaching for deep understanding, and put worry about the rubrics on hold temporarily.

Course Design

Having identified what I wanted them to learn, and what would count as a good job, it was important to be deliberate about how I was going to get there. In all of my teaching, it's important to me to be as *authentic and coherent* (Newmann, Smith, Allensworth, & Bryk, 2001) as possible, so that course experiences at the university can serve as models for teachers' professional practice. Borrowing from the example of master teachers Jane Hansen and Donald Graves, I don't ask my students to do anything I'm not willing to do myself; this is a useful way to make sure I'm not asking them to complete inauthentic exercises.

I very much want candidates to begin to identify as teachers (Gilrane, 2014) rather than as students, so I do all I can to *honor their voices as colleagues* (Margolis, 2009; Urzua & Vasquez, 2008; Wei, Darling-Hammond, Andree, Richardson, & Orphanos, 2009), beginning by asking them to address me as Colleen rather than as Dr. Gilrane. The opening assignment, a "Dear Colleen Letter," set up to invite them into a conversational dialogue with a colleague rather than an essay for a professor, is described in detail in chapter 2. My goal is that by creating an hospitable environment in which colleagues work on authentic tasks, I'll be providing opportunities for candidates' *engaged participation* (Hickey & Zuiker, 2005; Jurow, Tracy, Hotchkiss, & Kirshner, 2012) in developing the skills and habits of mind (Eisner, 2002) that should transfer later into whatever teaching settings they live and work.

I've already mentioned the importance of Jane Hansen and Donald Graves (Graves, 1985; Graves & Hansen, 1983; Hansen, 1983) to my own professional learning—as a longtime kindred spirit of theirs, I have long believed it to be my responsibility as a teacher to *meet my students where they are*, and help them grow from there, even before there were terms like *universal design principles* (CAST, 2011) or concepts such as *presumed competence* (Chandler-Olcott, Kliewer, & Petersen, 2010). Our program is working toward greater realization of these ideas, and the candidates enrolled in the spring block were comprised of both those working toward elementary licenses (including Hannah) and those working toward special educator licenses (including Jessica) as one effort to support the mutual development of teachers who might then more naturally work collaboratively in their careers (Pugach & Winn, 2011; Solis, Vaughn, Swanson, & McCulley, 2012). As one of the members of my teacher research group was a coteaching coach in the district in which our interns would be placed, I had arranged that she and her colleagues would visit one of our class meetings. I also knew I would make every attempt to incorporate universal design principles (CAST, 2011), with multiple ways for candidates to access, process, and represent their learning; however, given the real-world outcome toward which we would be working, they would in the end have to submit final written versions of their work, even if previous drafts needed to be completed in other media to support their success.

I was now in the same situation as any teacher waiting for the school year to begin. I knew what I wanted my students to learn and how I wanted them to demonstrate that learning. I had a framework for the ways I wanted to set up my classroom, and the things I wanted to ask my candidates to engage in to accomplish that learning. But I still needed for them to show up so that I could flesh out the details informed by who they were, what they cared about, knew already, and needed. What did we actually do once spring semester 2012 began?

IMPLEMENTING THE PLAN

As most instructors do in preparing for a new semester, I had immersed myself in materials related to our targeted content and practices, and had many, many ideas about ways to spend our three hours together each Friday morning. But try as I might, I just could not get the syllabus organized, and it took longer than it should have for me to realize that until I knew in more detail the answers to my own Essential Question #1—Who are my students? What do they care about? What do they know? What can they do? What kind of help do they need?—I could not know which, from all the many topics and engagements that might fill fifteen weeks, would be best. Neither could I know which ones needed more time, and which less. What I did know, with certainty, was that I wanted our last five weeks together (the time after spring break) to be a "workshop" in which candidates would be working on their learning plans with my being present to respond to their work in progress. All of my years as a writing teacher have taught me that there is no better opportunity for insight into how learners are making sense of what they are learning than when I pull up a chair and ask, "How's it going?" I did not want the learning plans to be a typical "course project" completed outside of class and then presented—I wanted the work on these to provide a laboratory for engaged participation (Hickey & Zuiker, 2005; Jurow et al., 2012) in the real-life work of planning for teaching, with expert mentoring and support available as needed. How else would I know what they were thinking?

My dilemma was in knowing how to organize the weeks before spring break to best help the candidates prepare for this workshop time, and I designed a new version of a written conversation I've used in other settings, the Dear Colleen letter (Gilrane, 2014). In the ELED 422 version of this assignment, I asked the candidates to "talk" with me about themselves—first as learners, and then as teachers—with respect to my four essential questions. This assignment is described in much detail in chapter 2, and the responses appear there and throughout the following chapters that describe our course. I was then able to use what I learned about my candidates in these letters to organize the course and select the materials, engagements, and other resources we would use. These are sketched broadly below, and discussed in more detail in the following four chapters, each of which focuses on one of the essential questions that provided our course framework.

Course Organization

On our first day together, we introduced ourselves and shared excitement over finally being in courses related to our mutual passion—teaching! Because our elementary candidates complete a baccalaureate degree in an arts and sciences major, they often feel as if they will never make it to their education courses, and are thrilled when that finally happens full time. I shared with them my poster board showing how the four essential questions "covered" all of the rubric items for TEAM and edTPA, and asked them to trust me enough to put their concerns (and in some cases, panic) on hold for now. I asked if they felt patronized by my believing that they needed in-class work time to work on learning plans, or if they wanted to devote that time to making presentations instead, and they expressed relief that they would not be expected to carry out this assignment entirely on their own. Knowing they might not all feel free to express anything else, I encouraged the ones whom I was meeting for the first time to "talk to your friends who have had my classes before." Fourteen of the twenty-seven candidates in our section had been, or were concurrently, my students in one or more literacy courses, and could share their perspectives and experiences with their colleagues.

I shared a timeline that was filled in for the first day—introductions and overview—had a topic for the following week—who are my students?—and then was blank until the five weeks after spring break when the workshop time was scheduled. I told them that before I could select topics or materials, or decide what to do with those nine weeks in between, I needed to know more about them, their concerns, needs, and strengths; the Dear Colleen letters were going to give me that information. They wrote these and posted them to Blackboard over the next four days, and the rest of the course schedule fell into place.

Models of Effective Teaching (2 weeks)

It was clear in the Dear Colleen letters that our class as a whole wanted to see examples of the kinds of excellent teaching they hoped to do themselves someday. One of the prompts I had asked them to respond to included the following: Have you ever seen this kind of teaching? Do you think you would recognize it? As you think about designing learning that meets all of these goals, and answers all of these questions, what do you want me to know? The responses made it clear that many of the candidates' own experiences had not allowed them to create a vision of engaged, thoughtful teaching and learning, much less how to achieve it; for example, Cameron wrote,

> I am not sure I have seen the kind of teaching shown in the handouts. If I have, then I have not recognized it. I have seen some teachers that have the goals for their students to acquire and make meaning, but not transfer. I am excited to learn more about these strategies and learn how to adequately use them to teach others.

VB also was unfamiliar, but unlike Cameron, she was apprehensive rather than excited:

> I have never seen this kind of teaching in this format. It looks like pieces are familiar, I have just never seen them together in this set up. After looking at set ups such as these, it just reinforces my nervousness for this class. I just really want to focus on learning how to set up my criteria the right way so that my teaching is not affected by all the standards and I am as organized as possible.

Julia and Claire F. explicitly requested examples, with Julia writing, *I want to see demonstrations and have more tip sheets on the different types of instruction*, while Claire F. wrote,

> So I think the most helpful thing for me would be to actually see a real-life teacher putting this into action. It is difficult for me to envision right now, especially with not much experience under my belt. Seeing it in person would help me make more sense of this process and confirm that it can be done and may not be as intimidating as it seems.

There were a few candidates who felt more comfortable in their ability to recognize and carry out this kind of teaching but who wanted to know more about how to integrate different content areas. Claire L. is an example of one of these who had already decided that one of the ways to deal with the myriad of content standards was to integrate them:

> I want to learn more about integrating content areas and creating a classroom in which the learning throughout the day, week, and school year ties together. It seems that the standards are so extensive that the only way to cover all of them is to cover multiple standards at one time by teaching broad concepts, processes, principles, and understandings. I would like to learn more about how to teach in ways that effectively encompass many standards at once.

I decided that using class time to "visit" exemplary classrooms together was worthwhile as (1) it would give us a common experience for discussion, and (2) I could not count on the field experience placements for accomplishing this with the necessary speed or with even quality. I was fortunate to have two VHS cassettes purchased years ago from Heinemann that are visits to Steven Levy's fourth-grade class in two different years, demonstrating his commitment to integrated, learner-focused instruction (Levy, 1996) that supports high-quality learning and production from students (Levy, 2000). The first video, "The Voyage of Pilgrims '92," showcased a year during which the pilgrims' voyage provided an overarching framework for the entire school year. Interviews with students a year after leaving the class, and interviews with parents and community members, were also included. The second video, "On the Path," described another year in which the history of the conversion of a no-longer-used railroad track to a bike path in their community became the theme that organized much of the year's work.

I designed what I called "think sheets" to serve as graphic organizers for candidates who wished to use them while viewing, focused on the four areas that had been patterns in their Dear Colleen letters as ones they wished to learn more about:

1. the teacher's role
2. the ways students demonstrated learning
3. integration of content areas
4. higher-order levels of thinking by students

Some of the candidates used these; others just sat and watched and needed more than one viewing to take it all in. Thanks to the excellent work of Dr. Renée Smith in our Office of Information Technology, these videos were digitized and made available to our class on Blackboard, after she talked with the publishers and then tracked down Mr. Levy, who graciously granted us this permission. Thus, candidates who wished to view them more than once

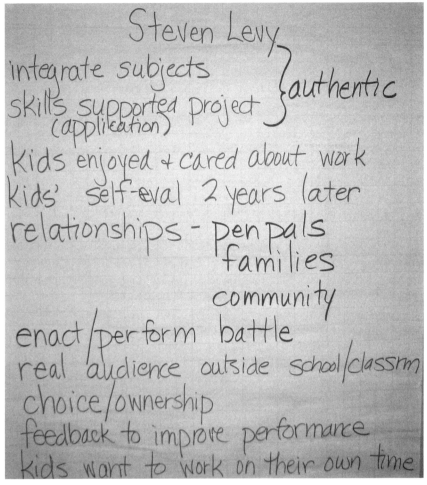

Figure 1.2.   Discussion Notes After Viewing Steven Levy's Classroom

could do so with ease. Figure 1.2 shows notes from an in-class discussion after viewing, and below are some reflections later posted to a discussion board after viewing.

The children were able to participate in these wonderful and knowledgeable projects, but also had subject areas that Mr. Levy had to make time for because the skills were not met during the projects. This would be a classroom that I would look forward to coming to everyday as a student. The children were able to interact with their community, interview and talk to different individuals, write letters, collect their own data, and construct new things. However, not only were the children getting things from their community, they were also giving back. I felt that these children learned so many different life lessons on top of the skills required through academics. . . . There was so much incorporated into these projects that allowed for the use of multiple learning styles. I liked being able to see the children's thoughts in the first video when they were interviewed a couple years after being in Mr. Levy's class. They all expressed how much they learned and enjoyed learning this way. A lot of the parents expressed how their child seemed so much more interested in what they were learning and enjoyed going to school every morning. This in return allows children to learn so much more. (Kim)

Kathleen valued some of the same things noticed by Kim, and added these specific observations:

I was particularly interested in how Mr. Levy was able to integrate so many of the content areas into the projects, quite seamlessly! What makes his approach so unique is how Mr. Levy values the process of learning naturally; developing skills, knowledge, and understanding by pursuing something that is meaningful and relevant to his students. By doing this he has allowed for an experience that is truly meaningful. . . . There were so many small things, too, that I loved about Steven Levy's way of teaching. When the students were writing letters to the abutters, Mr. Levy was reviewing them. When he found a few words that were misspelled he did not correct them in bright red ink, like we see so often, nor did he give them the correct spelling verbally. Instead, he circled the misspelled words and said, "See if you can find how to spell this word . . . and this one." So now the child must inquire how to spell and correct that word, perhaps using a dictionary. I love this because this is SUCH an important skill to teach children. As adults when we don't know something we can't immediately stop everything, throw up our hands, and say, "I don't know!" We have to say to ourselves "I'll find out!" Teaching children that they have the power to control their own knowledge by utilizing available resources is an important life skill.

Maree, a mom as well as a candidate, built on Kathleen's reflection to think about how this kind of teaching could fit the stated mission of the school her children attended:

I was truly amazed by Mr. Levy's classrooms represented in "The Voyage of Pilgrims '92" and "On the Path." Mr. Levy provided such a rich learning environment for his students and integrated so many subjects under the umbrella of a single theme or question. Levy's motivation was to "develop skills, knowledge and understanding in the course of pursuing something that was meaningful and relevant to the students." His goal of integration was to involve them so much in the curriculum that their interest was natural. In watching the videos, I couldn't help but think about the school my children attend and their mission statement that I imagine many schools echo of "preparing life-long learners and responsible, caring citizens." Mr. Levy gave his students such an opportunity in this type of preparation. For example, as Kathleen had mentioned, when Mr. Levy was reading the student letters to the abutters in "On the Path," he would circle the misspelled words and ask the students to find out how to spell it correctly. In doing this, he allowed the students to take on a responsible, active role in their learning. The students were involved in the process of questions, choices and experience in practicing skills needed to achieve and understand. An experience, as one parent mentioned, "of a lifetime" that would have life long effects. The students were given responsibility and took ownership of their learning. This was evident in their care and consideration to their desks, newsletters and research.

Alice's reflection homed in on the integration of content areas, the skills embedded in the bigger project goals, and the multiple ways of representing learning available to students:

These two projects were very realistic and helped students to understand real-life situations. There were various subjects included into these projects. From the outside most would not think that so many subjects and lessons would be included in these tasks, but when looking at the projects deeper it is amazing how many skills the students obtain each day. I know many young students that dread going to school or have a difficult time applying their work to solely paper and pencil, Mr. Levy's class definitely gives those students an opportunity to apply themselves in a completely different way.

Finally, VB, who had expressed such anxiety in her Dear Colleen letter, seemed to have that alleviated a bit by being presented with a vision of what's possible, even expressing enjoyment:

I have really enjoyed watching these videos. I find Levy to be a great influence for teachers of any subject and love how he can connect multiple subjects in one project or section of the year-long inquiry. The complexity that each project took on, the carpentry in "Pilgrims" and the "investigative" work for the path, was incredible for 4th grade students but they all seemed to enjoy it. It was as if he opened up so many doors for those children, such as a ton of hands-on experiences, getting a feel for many different types of jobs (reporting, investigating, carpentry) that some of them may have never experienced otherwise. He could have helped them find a hobby, passion, or even a future career during one of these projects. He has engaged them in a way that not many teachers have or ever will and I'm sure that is a nice break for the students to appreciate. I feel like his efforts probably gained him a lot of respect within his community as well as in his classroom. The amount of time he put into his lessons and gathering of materials for or resources for each project is a great example of how dedicated a teacher should be.

Who Are My Students? What Do I Want Them to Learn? (2 weeks)

These topics, as essential questions #1 and #2, are discussed extensively in chapters 2 and 3. While we devoted only two Fridays to them as explicit topics, they were woven into the candidates' experiences in many other ways throughout the semester, including the five weeks of workshop time designing the learning plans, their Monday content-focused classes, and the special education, educational psychology, and reading classes in the elementary education minor. The most important work we did with these essential questions on Fridays was attending to them in the design of the learning plans.

Assessment: What Would Count as a Good Job? (2 weeks)

We focused one Friday on performance assessment, and a second on formative assessment, as stand-alone topics; however, these were also present throughout the semester when I made my thinking public (Paris & Winograd, 2003) by pointing out that what I was attending to in an ongoing way, throughout the semester, was an example of formative assessment. As essential question #3, this is detailed in chapter 4, along with our course grading procedures.

What Resources Are Available to Me? How Do I Organize Them to Support Learning? (3 weeks)

Three Fridays were dedicated to essential question #4, discussed in depth in chapter 5. One week focused on materials, one on personnel and instructional strategies, and the third on time, space, environment, and pulling it together. As with the previous topics, resources were also discussed in the content classes, and were dealt with most importantly during the design of the learning plans.

Designing Your Learning Plans (5 weeks of workshop time)

Finally, after spring break, we reached the time we had been aiming toward since January, the designing and writing of learning plans! While we had five weeks devoted to this, there were only four class meetings, as one of the Fridays was the university's spring recess. Here is how this time was explained in the syllabus:

> I envision most of our time together in these weeks as a "workshop" during which you bring what you've been working on to share and receive feedback from me and from your colleagues. Bring with you the materials you need to work, including your laptop (if possible) so that you are able to access necessary websites. While I am listing each "step" in the process on a different

day, I expect that you will move at different rates and not necessarily all be doing the same thing at the same time. You will need your *Understanding by Design Professional Development Workbook* to guide your work.

Today you should have selected your content area and grade level. Bring with you to class the appropriate standards from the Tennessee DOE website.

Begin working on Stage 1: Desired Results.

Especially relevant sections of *Understanding by Design PD Workbook*: pp. 60–62, 68, 75, 77, 80, 83, 87.

Continue work on the learning plan, moving on to Stage 2: Evidence as you are ready.

Especially relevant sections of *Understanding by Design PD Workbook*: Overview: p. 197 (p. 180 is a nice self-assessment tool).

Generating Assessment Ideas: pp. 142, 145, 148, 151, 156, 164, 166.

Designing Assessment Tasks: 176, 172, 204, 205, 206.

Scoring Criteria for Evaluating Student Performance: 195, 187, 189, 190, 191, 192.

Continue work on the learning plan, moving on to Stage 3: Learning Plan as you are ready.
   Especially relevant sections of *Understanding by Design PD Workbook*: pp. 35–37; six-page template: pp. 46–51 (sample filled in pp. 52–57).

The three stages and their names are from the *Understanding by Design Professional Development Workbook* (McTighe & Wiggins, 2004) and align with essential questions #2, #3, and #4. The workbook contains many useful resources, forms, and graphic organizers to support teachers in thinking through the design of learning plans in a variety of ways, and many of our candidates chose to use some of these materials in their design processes. While using the materials in their designs was up to them, in the end they were all required to complete a self-evaluation of their plan using the "UbD Design Standards" included in the book, which invited them to consider five to seven indicators for each of the following questions:

Stage 1—To what extent does the design focus on the big ideas of targeted content?

Stage 2—To what extent do the assessments provide fair, valid, reliable, and sufficient measures of the desired results?

Stage 3—To what extent is the learning plan effective and engaging? (McTighe & Wiggins, 2004, p. 24)

Candidates knew that their plans needed to last at least three to five days, and could address the content of their choice at the grade level of their choice. They were free to work in teams of up to three people if they wished, and were responsible for writing one-day's plan in detail, using the official TEAM lesson plan form from the district in which they would be interning. They and I would both evaluate this lesson plan using the TEAM planning rubric, and compare results in a final evaluation conference.

These learning plans and lesson plans were the performance assessments I used to evaluate the candidates' learning and to provide for them engaged participation (Hickey & Zuiker, 2005; Jurow et al., 2012) in the practice of being a teacher. For some of them, just knowing they would be doing this instead of taking tests, and that they would have time built in to work on it, was critical to reducing stress, as HJ shared: *I really appreciated the planning workshop time in class to struggle, ask questions, and really think about what I was doing.* For others, such as Claire F., it was the opportunity to work collaboratively with a partner that seemed most beneficial:

> I did find the TEAM lesson plan to be more vague than I thought it would be, so that made it more difficult. However, conducting this authentic lesson plan finally got me thinking like a true teacher. The backwards design was extremely helpful because we first decided where we were going and then filled in the spaces with ways in which we would get there. We spent all three class days brainstorming and writing our ideas down and did not begin filling in the forms until we had developed the lesson on our own without these guides.

For me, this time was invaluable for the focused instruction I was able to do in conferences with candidates as they shared their work in progress with me. The biggest challenge that many of them faced in the beginning was wanting to begin their planning with materials and activities, rather than content and assessments. In conferences, I worked not to give them answers or tell them how to make everything fit, but to ask the questions that would help them find their own answers (Hansen, 2001) . . . and perhaps develop the habit of mind of asking these same questions in the future. So in a conference with someone who was trying to figure out how to use a certain children's book, or activity, or something else, I would ask them to remind me of their content goals and the understandings they wanted children to develop. I would ask them to share with me how they wanted their children to demonstrate their learning.

Sometimes, they had not completed these stages, and the "right answer" was clearly to do so. Sometimes, our conversations helped them clarify the place of the particular activity in their plan, and they could move on. But sometimes, it became clear that no matter how cute or fun or engaging a particular activity was, it really had nothing to do with the learning plan, and spending time on it was not going to move students toward satisfactory completion of the performance assessment. Kathleen and I had a number of conferences about her math unit—which was superb when it was finished, as her constant questioning of me and of herself was enormously productive. Here is how she reflected on it at the end of the semester:

> The learning plan—where should I begin? I will admit that I struggled with this. I realize now that this backwards design makes a lot of sense! I am not quite sure why I fought it for so long. I have the tendency to jump right into the activities. At first, I had an activity in mind that I knew I wanted to integrate. So I found myself trying to squeeze it into a standard—it wasn't fitting, but I still had a hard time letting go of it. Once I started focusing on who my students are, what I want them to know, and how I will measure their learning—instead of only on what I want them to do—it was much less of a struggle.

Conferences also provided opportunities to think with candidates about assessments, and to think past what is *easy* to measure to what is *important* to measure when we are thinking about content. Nancy and her partner had drafted a rubric for their unit on Culture that included items focused on neatness, timeliness, and behavior. We had spirited conversations about these issues. Were they important? Were they social studies content? Didn't students need to develop good work habits? I contacted my teacher colleagues who worked in the internship district, and one of them sent me a copy of the official report card, at which point we learned that while it included evaluations of work habits, it separated those from achievement grades in academic areas. Here is Nancy's final reflection on these issues

> How do I know/grade what a good job is? It does not mean their project is "pretty" or that they have stayed on task for the duration of the lesson. There is a place for these things, but it does not belong with the actual grade of their knowledge. Meeting the requirements of a rubric or the assigned requirements justifies knowledge. Nothing I assign will be able to be completed without a deeper understanding of the material. . . . We found that constructing the one in-depth TEAM lesson plan was pretty easy, but that the rubric was a little more difficult. After hearing your guidance, we were able to construct a strong rubric that matched our lesson.

Nancy and her colleague and I had a conference every single week, and I know that they were sometimes very frustrating for her as she just wanted me, as the expert, to *tell* her what she should do. And I continued to ask scaffolding questions to lead her to her own right answer, so that she'd be able to "have conferences with herself" (Hansen, 2001) when I and other mentors were not there in the future. I believe we were more on the same page by the end of the semester than we had been when we started, and I am encouraged by her giving informed consent to share her materials. I *know* from reading the reflection above that she did hard, thoughtful work on these issues, and pushed herself to grow.

Final Evaluation Conferences

When candidates work as hard as they do on these assignments, I want to give thoughtful responses to that work, and to have generative conversations about what's next, and what their plans might be for areas in which they still want to grow or are excited to learn more about. So rather than giving a final examination, I schedule thirty-minute final evaluation conferences with each person as the culminating experience for the course. These are discussed in detail in chapter 4 as essential question #3, What would count as a good job of learning?

Chapter Two

Question #1: Who Are My Students?

Early in my career, as a primary grade teacher yearning to know how better to support my students' language and literacy growth, I had the good fortune to attend International Reading Association meetings and to be exposed to the ideas of scholars whose work addressed this area. Prominent among them was Yetta Goodman, who coined the word *kidwatching* to name the kinds of observation teachers can do to inform their instruction so that is responsive to children's development. Here is how she talked about it:

> Good teachers, like Mr. Borton, have always been kidwatchers. The concept of kidwatching is not new. It grows out of the child study movement that reached a peak in the 1930s providing a great deal of knowledge about human growth and development. Teachers can translate child study into its most universal form: learning about children by watching how they learn. . . . The kidwatcher who understands the role of unexpected responses will use children's errors and miscues to chart their growth and development and to understand the personal and cultural history of the child. There are no tests available which can provide this kind of data to the professional educator. (Goodman, 1985, pp. 9, 13)

Yetta continues to refine and share her ideas (Goodman, 2011) while staying true to her core idea of learner-centered teaching; I cannot recommend her work highly enough. My own experiences over more than three decades as a teacher allow me to say two things with confidence:

1. Kidwatching is effective in teaching learners of any age, about any content (not only language).
2. One of the most effective ways to help teachers understand the power of kidwatching is to set up opportunities for them to experience it.

Thus, my first essential question for my candidates to embrace is, *Who are my students?* In this chapter I will show how we addressed this in ELED 422 from two perspectives, (1) the candidates themselves as my students, and (2) the candidates as teachers who need to be kidwatchers of their own students.

WHO ARE MY STUDENTS:
CANDIDATES AS COLLEEN'S KIDS

In regular classroom teaching, when I spent all day, five days a week, with my children, getting to know them did not take a great deal of time; even if that knowledge did deepen over time, I could learn enough to inform decision making fairly soon. There are times when consulting gives me the opportunity to get to know a school faculty over a long period of time as well, and these are experiences that lend themselves well to kidwatching. But most university courses meet once a week, for three hours, and if my instruction is to be responsive enough to my students as learners that they, in turn, are compelled to become kidwatchers themselves, something needs to happen to accelerate my learning about them. The Dear Colleen letter is one attempt at that acceleration.

The Dear Colleen Letter

Depending on the course, and its purpose, the Dear Colleen letter takes different forms, but it is always an attempt at collegial conversation rather than a formal essay; college students are already inventing the university (Bartholomae, 1985) more than enough in other settings. Requiring that the letters begin with the words *Dear Colleen* is something I began doing as a way to emphasize to my students that I was inviting them into an informal, personal discourse so that I might get their genuine thoughts rather than what they thought I was seeking as a "right answer" (Gilrane, 2014).

For our ELED 422, having shared with the candidates the four essential questions that I wanted to be our guides as we learned to plan instruction, it was important that I know their understandings of these concepts, as well as have insight into whom they were as learners themselves. I decided that talking about their own experiences and preferences as learners, in terms of the four questions, might help them value the utility of the questions themselves, as well as help me know my candidates. So for each of the four essential questions, I asked candidates to write two responses: one as learners, and one as teachers. For example, here are the prompts for question #1:

Essential Question #1: Who are my students? (What do they know? What can they do? What do they care about? What kind of help do they need?)

I'd like to know about you—please tell me what you want me to know about you *as a learner*. What do you know? What can you do? What do you care about? What kind of help do you need?

Now think about yourself *as a teacher*, who is wondering these same things about your own class: Who are my students? (What do they know? What can they do? What do they care about? What kind of help do they need?)

Share with me what you know about kids, what you don't yet know, and what you are concerned about. Are there certain kids you believe you will identify with and understand better than others? What do you think about that? What else do you want to share?

I learned a great deal from my candidates in their letters to me, about their knowledge and skills, cares and concerns (#1), what they want/need to learn (#2), how they wish—and do not wish—to have their learning evaluated (#3), and what types of assignments and engagements they believe work, and do not work, for them (#4). Much of this varied from individual to individual, and my responses needed to be personalized; however, there were patterns in the responses that were significant enough that I could make some decisions fairly quickly about ways of organizing our course. At the beginning of our second Friday meeting, I was able to share with the group these general observations about their learning preferences:

You want . . .

- visuals
- interesting readings
- time to plan
- group discussions
- to see examples
- to have explanations

You don't want . . .

- lectures
- boring readings
- to be put on the spot
- group grades/assignments

I told them that their letters indicated that while they brought different knowledge and experiences with them that led to their having different content needs, everyone in our class felt a need to build on their understanding of at least one of these overall concepts:

1. levels of student knowledge/understanding
2. forms of assessment
3. roles of the teacher for instructional goals
4. integration of instruction

I then explained how I had used this information about them when I created the four different "think sheets" that they might use to focus their viewing and/or note taking while visiting Steven Levy's class. Fortuitously, the video visits provided me with immediate opportunities to respond to their need to see examples while differentiating what they needed from those examples.

What Do My Candidates Care About?

As might be expected, all of my candidates care about children and about teaching well, and they shared their thoughts and feelings about those. Some went into more specific detail about what they cared about and/or why, such as this account from Bailey:

> I really care about passing on a love for learning. When I was a kid I never really loved school because I felt like it was boring. I do not want my kids to feel this way; I want them to come to school every day and love being there. . . . I care about keeping children safe and giving them a place to come and express themselves. I get overwhelmed with all of the testing and mandatory evaluations that are in place. You calmed me down a little the other day in class when you made a picture with the standards.

The privacy of the Dear Colleen letter allowed Ms. A to share her sense of a spiritual calling to the teaching of children with special needs:

> I care about many things, but, the things I care about most are children in general and those with special needs. This may sound odd, but I feel that God has chosen me to be a special education teacher. God has chosen me to help those with special needs become more independent and to endure less bullying in their lives. Mostly, I have always loved working with children with special needs because I feel that they need me.

Some candidates also take advantage of the opportunity to be present as human beings beyond their teacher/learner identities, such as in the case of

Elsie's sharing: *I love reading, spending time with my friends, being silly and listening to music.*

What Kinds of Help Do My Candidates Need?

Dear Colleen letters help me learn a great deal about classroom structures and specific strategies that candidates find to be necessary to support them as learners. Sometimes, writers also give me specific advice about responses they will need from me when they encounter difficulties.

Classroom/Course Structures

Letters often reflect as much about previous learning situations that did not work as they do about the writers themselves. By the time they get to their education courses, some of our candidates are more than ready to be treated as the professionals they are preparing themselves to be, as HJ expressed:

> When I need help with something I like to have the freedom and security to ask the teacher and/or fellow students in a conversational manner—I do not like when teachers expect students to know everything. An annoyance of mine as a student is when the entire class is confused, and the teacher blames the students rather than him or herself. . . . I suppose that overall, I appreciate being treated like an adult rather than a child. I have found that the classes that have had the greatest impact on me have been set up as safe environments where everyone is treated as an adult and we are all interested in learning more about what we are studying.

Claire L. expressed a need to know what to expect, with time for thinking and processing and writing:

> When it comes to learning, I'm a thinker and a planner. I need time to process and reflect on what I'm learning. It always takes me longer than everyone else, but it's worth it to feel like I did it right.

Specific Strategies

By the time they are juniors or seniors in college, candidates have had many opportunities to identify situations in which they need support as learners, and sometimes to identify the strategies that are the most helpful. I learned of a strategy Julia used to help her focus, and that she wanted me to be aware of so that I did not think she was off task:

When I am in class the way I best learn is by writing things down and doodling. It may seem that doodling around notes would take away from learning, and be distracting. However, in my case I feel as though I am more engaged and attentive when I am writing notes or doodling.

Allie identified not only a challenging type of assignment but also a strategy she was beginning to find useful, that she had learned about in her reading education class:

I am also a very visual learner. I prefer drawing outlines and diagrams, so that I can visualize certain relationships and better understand the concepts. I have a very difficult time being assigned readings from a textbook, mostly because I have a difficult time understanding the information and usually have a hard time focusing. However, I have already learned how important it is to have a purpose for reading, so I have begun to approach my textbooks differently, trying to understand what I am reading and the importance of it. A few things that will help me to learn will be to make sure that assignments are very clear and also to use as many visuals as possible, instead of large amounts of textbook reading (which I know you are not fond of anyways!).

Both of these letters, and others like them, alerted me to behaviors I might observe in my classroom and helped me know the meaning assigned to them by the candidates themselves. Allie's letter also gave me insight into another important outcome of these letters, clues to how to respond when certain difficulties are encountered.

Responses My Candidates Need from Me

Dear Colleen letters often express frustration with the not-differentiated nature of many college courses, and share specific responses that would be useful from me in particular situations. Kelly let me know I might need to draw her out by writing, *I tend to be on the quiet side, so it will take a little more effort for me to speak up in class.* Sylvia went further, challenging the assumption that the only way to be engaged in a class is by speaking:

I have had classes in the past where you lost points if you didn't make a thought-provoking statement or ask a thought-provoking question in class. Although I am fairly outgoing, I have never been the student to want to speak up frequently in front of the whole class. I hate getting answers wrong and I hate voicing my wrong answer to a big group of people. With that being said, I really enjoy small-group discussions. I think the intimacy of the setting minimizes the anxiety I have speaking in front of my peers/colleagues.

Often, I learn that the structures in place to allow students to draft, receive responses, and revise their work—without loss of points or lowering of grades—are welcomed, as in this letter from Sarah:

> I learn in a variety of ways. I am a more visual learner than auditory learner. I learn well when I understand what I did wrong and have a chance to redo and rethink after constructive criticism. I think your class will actually be a perfect fit for me. I need a teacher who is willing to explain things when I don't understand and be patient with me.

How Do My Candidates Want/Need to Be Assessed? To Be Taught?

The sections of the Dear Colleen letters in which the candidates talked about themselves as learners with respect to questions #3 and #4 provided me with many opportunities to model differentiation, as there was enormous variety in their expressed preferences for the types of assignments they found useful and the types of assessment they believed showcased them as learners. I hope in the sections and chapters that follow to demonstrate how I attempted to build in that differentiation.

As shared above, there were a few areas of consensus; requests not to have lectures or boring readings presented no surprises. Allie stated above that she knew I was not fond of large amounts of textbook reading; she knew this from having previously been enrolled in my reading education course. I want children to have opportunities to read real books rather than basal readers, and I will not use methods textbooks because I see them as basal readers for adults. By using professional articles and books in my courses, I am staying true to my commitment not to ask my students to do anything I'm not willing to do myself, as well as providing them opportunities for engaged participation (Hickey & Zuiker, 2005; Jurow, Tracy, Hotchkiss, & Kirshner, 2012) in an authentic professional learning activity that can go with them into their careers. So their requests for *interesting readings* were ones I received gladly!

The consensus around group work was fascinating, as they clearly valued the learning that took place during group discussion but wanted no part of being assigned group work to be graded. I selected excerpts from two letters that are typical of the responses on this issue. Rose wrote, *I do enjoy group work but find myself doing a lot of the work to make up where others are lacking*, while Julia shared,

> I have always had a love-hate relationship with group work. When I have part-
> ners who work equally hard it seems to be an accurate demonstration of knowl-

edge on everyone's behalf. However, sometimes it isn't that ideal. I do enjoy working with classmates and getting to know their understandings and opinions.

You will notice in the sections and chapters that follow that we often worked in small groups during our nine weeks of preparing to write learning plans, but that these were self-selected groups, without graded assignments. When it came to the learning and lesson plans themselves, it was up to each candidate to decide whether to work individually or as part of a team of two or three. This ability to choose afforded some of them the quality control they needed to make group work a productive option.

WHO ARE MY STUDENTS: CANDIDATES WATCHING *THEIR* KIDS

Our candidates have many opportunities throughout their preparation program to think about the diverse needs of the children they will be teaching. All of their content-focused classes—the reading education course in the minor, the Mondays during the spring block, and the graduate courses they will take in math, science, social studies, and literacy methods—address development with respect to that content and strategies for differentiation with respect to culture, race, economic status, language, and ability. In their special education course in the minor, they complete an assignment that they refer to as "my UDL," a lesson plan following a Universal Design for Learning format.

Addressing Diversity in Our Friday Classes

My job, on Fridays, was to help them think about how to pull together what they were learning in all of these places and apply it as teachers. This was addressed in a variety of ways—first, I tried, throughout the semester, to make explicit the ways in which I was working to build in responses to my candidates, and differentiation when necessary, in everything we did. Then, I would raise the issue of transfer—how might they, in their own teaching, borrow my strategy, or accomplish what I had tried to do? How might this look in a real elementary classroom?

Conferences Addressing Diversity during Workshop Time

The five weeks of workshop time provided rich opportunities to think with candidates about enacting differentiation in the learning plans they were designing. In a conference discussing a plan that included work and materials provided at home, I might ask, *how are you going to ensure that children whose parents are working after school, or whose families cannot afford these materials, have opportunities to learn?* Discussing a plan that might not be a literacy-focused lesson but that relied heavily on writing for representing learning, I might ask, *what about kids for whom writing is not a strength? Will you able to tell if it's science knowledge they are missing, or if their writing ability is not allowing them to show you what they've learned?*

When children's literature was to be built into these plans, it was often necessary to talk in conferences about the difficulty of the text, or the background knowledge required to understand it (which might differ from various cultural or economic perspectives), or whether it reinforced negative stereotypes. These conversations might lead to solutions such as deciding to present the books differently (read aloud rather than children reading independently), or to inviting guest speakers to share cultural background, or to selecting additional books to support the presentation of multiple perspectives, or— sometimes—to deciding not to use a particular book for a particular purpose.

Class Session Addressing Diversity as a Stand-Alone Topic

While the conferences about their work-in-progress learning plans were without doubt the most productive instances of learning to address diverse needs, we did have one Friday class meeting before that during which we dealt with diversity as a stand-alone topic. Knowing from the Dear Colleen letters that my candidates varied in their knowledge and experiences with diverse learners, and wanting to allow for differentiation to support that, I identified eight different articles (all of which, I hoped, represented "interesting readings") to help focus our discussion. Included among these articles were different elements of what a synthetic review of literature identified as the instructional dimension of culturally responsive pedagogy:

1. Acknowledge students' differences as well as their commonalities.
2. Validate students' cultural identity in classroom practices and instructional materials.
3. Educate students about the diversity of the world around them.
4. Promote equity and mutual respect among students.
5. Assess students' ability and achievement validly.
6. Foster a positive interrelationship among students.
7. Motivate students to become active participants in their learning.
8. Encourage students to think critically.
9. Challenge students to strive for excellence as defined by their potential.
10. Assist students in becoming socially and politically conscious. (Richards, Brown, & Forde, 2007)

Table 2.1. Selection of Readings Addressing Diversity

Article	Disciplines Addressed	Type of Diversity Addressed	Number of Dimensions Addressed
Richards et al. (2007)	general	culture + special needs	10
Browder et al. (2008)	literacy	special needs	4
Carrier, S. J. (2009)	STEM	gender	8
López-Robertson et al. (2010)	general, + social science	racial linguistic ethnic economic	7
MacGillivray et al. (2010)	literacy social science	economic	9
Miles, K. (2012)	general, especially literacy	special needs linguistic	9
Pang et al. (2011)	literacy STEM social science	racial linguistic ethnic	10
Roth, L. (2012)	literacy physical education	special needs	6

As seen in table 2.1, each of the articles addressed at least four of these dimensions, with most addressing six or more. They also dealt with different content areas, and various forms of diversity. I am not necessarily endorsing this list of articles (which can be found at the end of this section) for anyone else's use; indeed, I would update it myself over time in response to new candidates' needs and as new, excellent articles are published. I offer it simply as an example of a set of readings that addresses multiple dimensions. I also point out that two were online media rather than print-based articles, making them more preferred for some candidates.

To prepare for our class meeting, I asked the candidates to select two articles to read ahead of time, representing two different categories of diversity. When they arrived, they found five pieces of chart paper on the walls, labeled Racial Diversity, Ability Diversity, Economic Diversity, Language Diversity, and Gender Diversity. Their task was to self-select into small groups and discuss what they had read, with the goal of sharing suggestions with other teachers about strategies for dealing with each type of diversity. I was explicit about their task being to give advice to other teachers, so that they were required to synthesize what they'd read in different articles and to share their understandings rather than to give a book-report style presentation of what they'd read. Each group was also responsible for deciding on a plan for sharing in the whole group: Would one person present the list? the whole

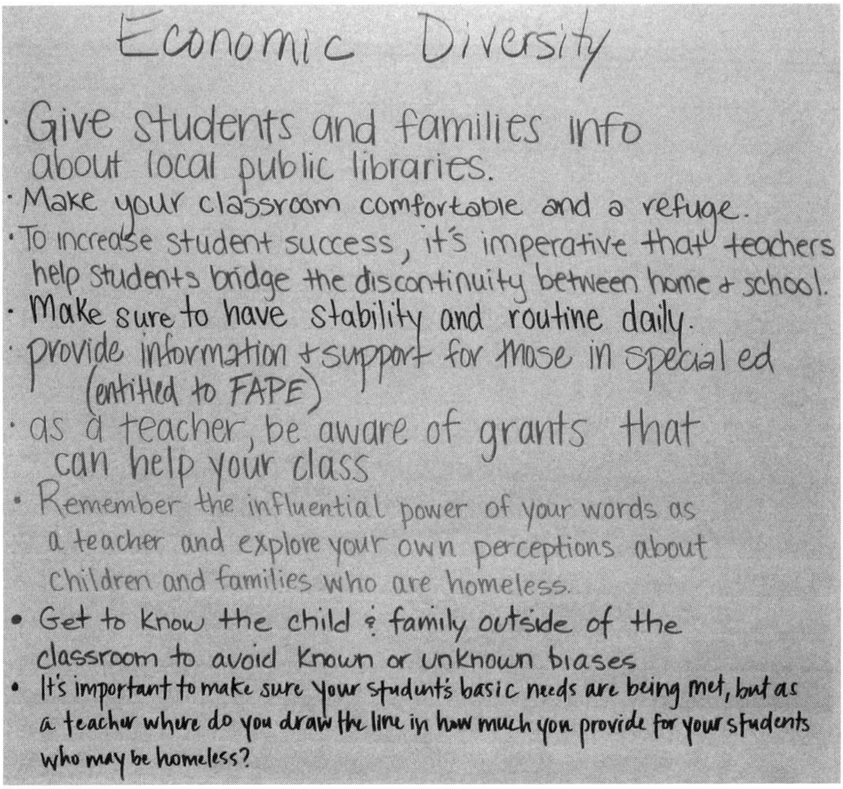

34 *Chapter Two*

Figure 2.1. Candidates' Advice for Addressing Economic Diversity

group? In this way I made sure no one was put on the spot before the whole class, and that those who needed it had rehearsal time.

A sample chart from one group, the one addressing economic diversity, can be seen in figure 2.1. I moved from group to group, listening in and occasionally participating in conversation, as they were working. The presentations led to productive whole-group conversations in which most candidates participated after having the opportunity to practice in small groups. I was especially pleased when a group's presentation led to others in the class wanting to know which specific article was being referenced so that they could look to it for ideas. Technology in the form of cell phone cameras made it simple to post these charts on Blackboard for all to consult later, if desired.

The list of articles we read to inform these conversations is below.

Browder, D. M., Mims, P. J., Spooner, F., Ahlgrim-Delzell, L., & Lee, A. (2008). Teaching elementary students with multiple disabilities to participate in shared stories. *Research & Practice for Persons with Severe Disabilities, 33*, 3–12.

Carrier, S. J. (2009). Environmental education in the schoolyard: Learning styles and gender. *Journal of Environmental Education, 40* (3), 2–12.

López-Robertson, J., Long, S., & Turner-Nash, K. (2010). First steps in constructing counter narratives of young children and their families. *Language Arts, 88* (2), 93–103.

MacGillivray, L., Ardell, A. L., & Curwen, M. C. (2010). Supporting the literacy development of children living in homeless shelters. *Reading Teacher, 63*, 384–92.

Miles, K. (2012). Jacob Artson, LA teen with autism, communicates through typing. Huffington Post, January 12, 2012. http://www.huffingtonpost.com/2012/01/12/jacob-artson-teen-autism-typing_n_1184950.html.

Pang, V. O., Stein, R., Gomez, M., Matas, A., & Shimogori, Y. (2011). Cultural competencies: Essential elements of caring-centered multicultural education. *Action in Teacher Education, 33*, 560–74.

Richards, H. V., Brown, A. F., & Forde, T. B. (2007). Addressing diversity in schools: Culturally responsive pedagogy. *Teaching Exceptional Children, 39* (3), 64–68.

Roth, L. (2012). Florida parents seek help from special education advocates. *Orlando Sentinel*, January 2, 2012. http://www.orlandosentinel.com/os-florida-special-education-advocacy-20111225,0,4028836.story.

WHO ARE MY STUDENTS: WHAT DID CANDIDATES LEARN?

In their final evaluation letters, most of the candidates wrote about having a heightened awareness of the importance of knowing their students well, even if they had thought of this as necessary to start with. For example, VB wrote,

> To address the first question, "Who are my students?" I would initially have said, "Oh, that's easy, that just means knowing what your students like." However, I have learned that it is much more than that. It is considering that they like, but being able to take that and put it into a lesson to engage as many students as possible. It is also knowing how your students learn. In order to truly teach our students, we have to know if they learn best by writing notes, if they learn best by hands-on activities, or if they need visual/hearing aids or any other kind of adjustment.

Cathie described her growth away from essentializing group characteristics, as well as her increased sensitivity to certain types of diversity:

> I must realize that things are never universals because every student is going to be unique. Being able to recognize the diversity within my classroom will help me be a better teacher who is able to differentiate. . . . While exploring this question, I particularly became more aware of students who are English language learners, homeless, or have a disability. I also learned that it is important to find out what our students' interests are so that we can know how to effectively motivate them.

I am always grateful when I learn that candidates have moved past certain unhelpful stereotypes, especially those pervasive in the media that blame parents for children's achievement or lack thereof. Sarah's reflection is one such example:

> Knowing my students also includes knowing their background, family situation, accommodation needs and being sensitive to each. I will be aware that not all families have resources, like a computer or even books, at home. I will be aware that just because parents do not show up to meet with me, it doesn't mean they don't care. . . . It is important to keep in mind that not all families are raised the same, think the same, value things the same, or act the same way as I do. That is what makes up who we are.

Occasionally, candidates reflect on the specific things that provoked their changed thinking, as in Bailey's reflection on my not fleshing out the syllabus before the Dear Colleen letters:

> In the beginning, I was thinking well of course I need to know my students, but I never really thought about how in-depth that knowledge could be. After seeing the way you conducted our class at the beginning of the semester, with regards to the syllabus, I really began to see that I need to know their backgrounds, their learning style, what makes them feel comfortable, as well as what makes them feel uncomfortable. I now see that I should not force my students to conform one way or another. I want them to be individuals. My job as the teacher is to make sure that I am planning a path for success for my students. I want them to feel comfortable in the classroom because if they are not comfortable, they will not have the confidence to succeed.

Finally, Christine shared that after my making my thinking public (Paris & Winograd, 2003) made her aware of how I was differentiating in our class, she began to notice differentiation in some of her other classes:

> I know in every education class they speak of differentiated learners and how you need to meet the needs of all students, but it was not until this semester that I really began to take notice of it. I really appreciate how you attempted to meet everyone's individual needs while still meeting the needs of the class. I also began to notice in my other classes how professors would do certain things that they wouldn't state why they were doing, but it was clearly an attempt to meet the needs of others. For example, I would take a mental note when a professor would use different colors between topics for visual learners, or would allow others to record their lectures for later listening.

What a kidwatcher! What a great lens she is developing to take into her internship year, when she will work alongside a mentor who is an exemplary teacher!

Chapter Three

What Do I Want Them to Learn?

> Perhaps one of the greatest challenges in teaching is creating intersections between the concerns of children and those of content. Continuously interweaving the demands of the subject matter with the needs of the students so as to shape the curriculum toward the child and the child's interests toward the curriculum is rather like sculpting a double helix of teaching and learning. (Darling-Hammond, 2006b, p. 189)

While we place a high value on teacher content knowledge in our program, we've never believed that front-loading all of that content was as important as our candidates' developing knowledge-in-use (Wittgenstein, 1953) with respect to content, hoping to support the development of the very phenomenon Darling-Hammond describes in this quote. Before the full-year graduate internship, our candidates will have taken an introductory reading methods course, and the introductions to math, science, and social studies methods in the Monday meetings of ELED 422. More substantive engagements are built into the internship year itself, when they take two of their four required graduate methods courses on Friday mornings after teaching all day Monday through Thursday. The other two courses are taken when they fit the candidate's program—either the summer before, or the summer after, internship, unless they happened to have room in their schedules to take a graduate course or two under a "senior privilege" provision that the university has for seniors with strong enough academic records to begin graduate study.

So my goal in our Friday meetings was not content expertise, but rather to support the development of a disposition to bring together knowledge of students, knowledge of content, and commitment to fostering deep, enduring understandings. Indeed, the title of this section of the syllabus was, *What do I want them to learn? Connecting my students to curriculum standards.*

The candidates spent Monday mornings with content specialists, being introduced to standards, best practices, materials, and professional organizations. In our Friday meetings, the most productive attention we paid to content was while the candidates were designing their learning plans, and spending time at Stage 1 determining what was worth learning, which skills and knowledge could be subsumed under which concepts and understandings, and how all of these might relate to any particular group of students. Especially for those who selected literacy or mathematics areas, where there are many skills as well as concepts, this provided an opportunity for grappling with these challenging issues, as Maggie reflected in her final letter:

> Bailey and I struggled the most with finding the essential questions of our unit and lesson plan. We chose a mathematics lesson on algebra, specifically multiplication. This obviously is a skill, so we had to look at it in a different context than a lesson in science or social studies.

Sarah, who chose a literacy focus, shared similar struggles:

> When I started to choose a standard I was trying to do a lesson on some standards that should not be taught [by themselves]. Through a conference with you I realized how a lot of the standards are crucial skills for the students to have, but not skills that I should do a unit lesson on. I kept these standards in mind so that I could integrate them into my lesson of elements of a story.

SPECIFIC SUPPORTS FOR THINKING ABOUT CONTENT

While the work-in-progress conferences with candidates were the most important sites for productive attention to dealing with content, there were two specific engagements built in to our course to support development in this area. We spent one class session focused on content as a stand-alone topic, and I introduced the candidates to the concept of backward planning from the Understanding by Design framework (McTighe & Thomas, 2003; McTighe & Wiggins, 2004; Wiggins & McTighe, 2005).

Class Session Addressing Content as a Stand-Alone Topic

Our Friday stand-alone session related to content included some procedures similar to our diversity session, as well as others that varied. In preparation for class, candidates were to read a piece describing the experiences of a novice teacher attempting to enact a culturally responsive curriculum (Bergeron, 2008). I believed that her struggles would relate to their concerns already expressed about these issues, and I asked the class to think of it as a visit to the teacher's classroom. I also wanted them to go to the Tennessee Department of Education website and download the Tennessee Academic Vocabulary guide, so that we could review and critique it together and discuss constructive ways to accomplish its goals. To support this, I provided three different pieces (articles or reports) focused on academic language and suggested that they select and read one to familiarize themselves with the concept. Remember, other classes were also addressing content!

The meat of preparation for this day, however, was for them to select a content area, and a grade/age level, and familiarize themselves with the standards and the professional organizations and other resources available to them. Here are the instructions from the syllabus for this class session:

1. Visit Christina's room by reading the Bergeron piece.
2. Visit the DOE website, click on the "academic language," link and download the Tennessee Academic Vocabulary guide.
3. Select one of the articles on academic vocabulary and read it to get an idea of what this is about.
4. Select a content area and dive into the standards, with the ideas of
   • becoming familiar with them, and
   • considering how to relate them to your students. Ask yourself,
5. What content is there?
6. Why should students care about it?
7. How can I help different students relate to, access, and process their learning?
8. Consider the resources available to you from professional organizations, from our state department of education, and from CAST as you think about connecting your students to these curriculum standards.

URLs were provided for the State Department of Education and CAST, and the names of the relevant content-focused professional organizations were listed so that candidates could carry out searches to find their websites and their recommendations.

Our class meeting itself was very similar to the diversity class, although it did begin with a whole-class discussion on the Bergeron article, which elicited sympathy from the students as well as affirming for them that they were not the only ones with these concerns. Then they formed into groups that had selected the same content/grade level range; for example, primary grade math, intermediate grade reading, and more, and discussed what they had learned so far about instruction. The background knowledge varied widely across the content areas, as some students had taken more courses than others, and our own group was still in its first five-week content cycle on Mondays, so that there were two areas in which they were on their own! But given that my goal was building habits of mind rather than mastery, this was time well spent. Groups that were less than satisfied with what they knew at this point were able to go into their later content courses with clear learning goals and questions they wanted answered! We wrapped up with each group sharing its advice; the chart from the group focused on primary grade social studies is shared as an example in figure 3.1.

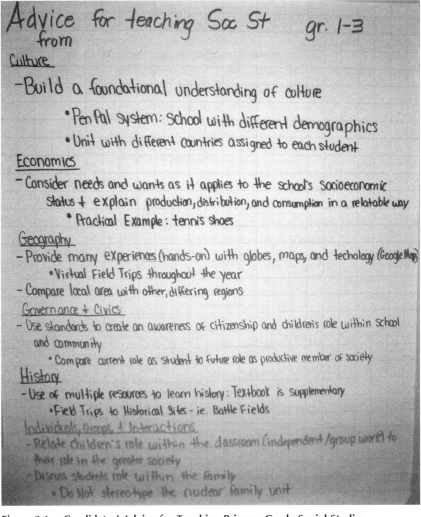

Figure 3.1.   Candidates' Advice for Teaching Primary Grade Social Studies

The Understanding by Design Framework

The Understanding by Design (UbD) framework developed by Grant Wiggins and Jay McTighe is built on what they call "backward planning," by which they mean, it is necessary to identify where you want to end up before you can begin (McTighe & Thomas, 2003; Wiggins & McTighe, 2008). They suggest that a remedy for the tendency to obsess about standardized test performance is to look back to the big ideas underlying content standards:

> Understanding key concepts and searching for answers to provocative questions—essential questions that human beings perennially ask about the world and themselves—should be the primary goals of teaching and learning. Students' understanding of the key ideas embedded in the content standards, then, should be the focus of any school improvement initiative. While seeking answers to important questions, students learn specific facts, concepts, and skills—those that typically appear on standardized tests—in the context of exploring and applying the larger ideas. (McTighe & Thomas, 2003, p. 52)

As a literacy educator, I've had many experiences teach me how crucial it is to define the goal, and what counts as a good job of it, before latching on to instructional activities. In fact, the second class meeting of the introductory reading education course in the elementary education minor is titled, What We Are Working Toward: Independent, Fluent, Strategic Reading. I want to establish right away that having our eyes on an appropriate target is critical when making instructional decisions; for example, with that goal in mind, I'll never engage children in practicing decoding of pseudo words. In preparing for engaging this idea more broadly in ELED 422, when thinking about planning in general, the best discussions I found of it were around the UbD framework. What I like best about their *Understanding by Design Professional Development Workbook* (McTighe & Wiggins, 2004) is that it provides prompts for thinking, rather than scripts to follow.

The workbook contains an array of examples and supporting graphic organizers presented in a variety of formats. Candidates who choose to use these materials to help them think through their design are able to choose resources that support their particular style of learning and processing as well as their selected content. We looked together at their example of the U.S. History topic of World War II (McTighe & Wiggins, 2004, p. 66), and the filled-in graphic organizer helped the candidates recognize the differences between principles and generalizations, concepts and processes, and discrete skills and factual knowledge. There are other examples to consult if needed, but most useful were the blank graphic organizers, and candidates were directed to these while they were working on Stage 1 of their learning plans.

WHAT DO I WANT THEM TO LEARN: WHAT DID CANDIDATES LEARN?

In thinking about what the candidates had learned by the end of the semester, I looked at both their learning and lesson plans and their final reflection letters. Important growth had occurred in the areas of connecting students to content, of identifying appropriate content goals, and of slowing down "coverage" to take the time to learn deeply.

Connecting Students to Content

The products themselves—the learning plans and lesson plans—reflected candidates' attention to curriculum standards and connecting those to students. Borrowing words from the quote at the beginning of this chapter, our candidates had all begun sculpting the double helix. Many addressed this explicitly in their final letters. Here are a few examples, starting with VB, who wrote, *being able to incorporate instruction so that your standards are understood by each student is one of the most important factors of teaching.* Michelle elaborated a bit more, writing:

> What do you think is important to them or important for them to know for later grades or just life in general; that's what you want them to learn. You want them to learn about useful and interesting subjects or skills, and things that they are interested in. I know that you still have to follow standards and guidelines, but that doesn't mean you can't find ways to engage them and make it interesting and make them want to learn.

Rose actually wrote a paragraph merging essential questions #1 and #2 explicitly, and relating children to the state curriculum standards:

> My development in understanding our four big topics was supplemented by the field experience observations. The one big thing I am taking with me from my education courses is how important it is to get to know your students. You have to know their likes, interests, and how they learn so you can show them that you care and develop lesson plans to help each child learn to the best of their ability. Visiting and revisiting TN standards has helped me see some of the things we will be covering as teachers. This falls under what we want our students to learn. I want my students to know I care and I want them to learn a lot from my teaching. I want to incorporate interesting activities and performance tasks so they can learn through authentic experiences.

The Process of Identifying Content Worth Learning

Some of the candidates explicitly addressed the planning process as helping them think deeply about content, even when it was challenging. Claire F. wrote,

> In thinking about what I want my students to learn, I think the biggest idea that is sticking with me from this class is how we did the backward designed lesson plan. What I want my students to learn should be the anchor of any lesson. This way of thinking, by using the lesson's standards to plan the assessment first, is something I had not thought about before but something I want to take into planning every lesson. Also, as I decide what it is I want them to learn, I want there to be multiple ways that my students can display good learning.

Many candidates agreed about the utility of the process, and expressed that it was challenging at first but that the work that went into identifying learning goals paid off in making later steps in the process clearer. Here's how Adalee talked about it:

> It was hard to come up with the enduring understandings and transferable ideas. However, once I was done with that, the rest seemed to fall into place. I was able to come up with questions that asked for more than recall. I have a feeling that the "Questioning for Understanding" page will be by my side when I plan future lessons. . . . I can see where it would be easy to ask and teach superficial facts. However, what is the point of teaching if students do not develop an understanding of why they have to learn something?

Maggie related a story that made me laugh, imagining her coworker's reaction, at the same time that it made me appreciate that she was already applying aspects of the process to other parts of her life:

> I recognize that you must have asked yourself, "What are my essential questions?" as you prepared to help us discover what our essential questions were for this course. I hope I can articulate this well; what I mean to say is I think in your planning of this course, you must have sat down and confirmed that your targeted understandings for us were enduring and transferable. I say this because I literally found myself asking a friend at work, "Well, what is our essential question?" See, we were preparing our marketing project for this summer, as the telefund is looking for sponsors for next year. My colleague had identified prospective donors. Through careful planning, he could easily provide extensive information to them about who we were and what we wanted. However, he had left out what I determined to be our essential question: why should businesses give to us? It made me think about what I have learned about planning a lesson—about how crucial conveying the "why" of a lesson really is. I hope this connection between what I have learned about teaching students and what I

have already applied to other areas of my life is as powerful to you as it is for me. I now understand the purpose and design of essential questions and see the relevance beyond the realm of school.

The Importance of Depth over Coverage

Another powerful connection that it was possible for us to make—and that the candidates appreciated—was how well the planning process might fit with Common Core State Standards, which were beginning to be rolled out in some content areas in our state. Sylvia noted in her final letter, *I think I have scheduled a small amount of depth in a large amount of time*, and Kim described her and Alice's work this way:

> As Alice and I were first starting to put things together, we were a little ambitious about what we wanted to get done. We quickly learned that it is more important not to try to do too much, but to incorporate meaningful activities that go more in depth in the material. This will provide our students with a deeper understanding.

In conferences with these and other candidates as they encountered similar problems in their designs, it was a relief for them to realize that this planning process would not need to be abandoned when new standards were introduced; in fact, it would fit them better than much of what was current practice in the schools.

Chapter Four

Question #3: What Would Count as Evidence of Learning?

Teachers must have in mind what will count as a good job of learning in order to be aiming at the right target in their instructional decisions and formative assessments. Spending time thinking about authentic performance assessments that "put understanding first" (Wiggins & McTighe, 2008) before planning instructional activities is a crucial habit of mind for our candidates to develop. It can be an especially challenging one after years of experiences of high school courses designed for passing tests, and college courses giving points for attendance and "class participation" that might include reading aloud from PowerPoint slides. The idea of evaluating *learning itself* is often a new one for many candidates.

I believe that this is the essential question that was best demonstrated for the candidates by their experiences in our Friday class, as there were no tests, nor points assigned to weekly assignments or class participation or other tasks. Everything we did was aimed at the same target: their successful designing of learning plans and lesson plans aimed at teaching for deep understanding that would also satisfy TEAM requirements. My strategy of making my thinking public (Paris & Winograd, 2003) got more mileage here than anywhere else, as I made explicit for the candidates everything I was learning about them along the way from formative assessments. Candidates' development in assessment was supported by our course assessment and grading procedures, by two class sessions devoted to assessment as a stand-alone topic, and of course, most productively, by their design of the assessment portions of their learning plans, supported by the UbD framework (McTighe & Wiggins, 2004) and the workshop time in class.

LEARNING ABOUT ASSESSMENT BY BEING ASSESSED

For a kidwatcher (Goodman, 1985), the many opportunities I had to observe and to interact with my candidates while they worked in small groups, or later while they designed their learning plans in workshop, were like a gold mine of information to be interpreted! And our final evaluation and grading procedures were part of my effort to demonstrate to them that engaged participation in authentic activities (Hickey & Zuiker, 2005; Jurow, Tracy, Hotchkiss, & Kirshner, 2012) was a legitimate form of assessment, and did not preclude successful performance on more surface-level assessments (Wiggins & McTighe, 2008).

Formative Assessment of My Candidates

The course design, influenced as it was by what I learned about my class in the Dear Colleen letters and from my ongoing observations, was a demonstration of using assessment data to inform instruction. What I needed to do was make all of this explicit for the candidates.

During those class meetings when we had small groups that discussed topics and/or readings and then reported out by sharing with the rest of us, I spent the small group time wandering from group to group, listening, sometimes interacting, and making notes, both mental and written. I noted insights, questions, concerns, misconceptions—whatever seemed important to the learning of individuals or groups. Sometimes on-the-spot intervention was needed, if something was really so far wrong that it would derail a group's work, or if they asked directly for help. Most of the time I waited.

Later, either at the end of that class or the beginning of the next, I would present and discuss a list of "general observations," or share some information or resources that it seemed to me the entire class needed to know about. I always told them that (1) my decision to share these notes or information or resources was based on what I'd observed in their group discussions and/ or presentations. Then, once the information itself was shared and seemed understood, I would tell them that (2) what I was demonstrating was formative assessment.

I was able to do the same thing with discussion board postings, written assignments (like the Dear Colleen letter and other times when I polled for information), and, of course, the in-progress learning plans during workshop. Most often, unless we ran out of time, I'd share the observations and issues at the end of the session in which I'd collected the data, and share the resources at the beginning of the next. If the resources were electronic, I could share in between classes and use email to remind them what I was responding to with the materials.

By the end of the semester, I'd made explicit the range of things I'd paid attention to in order to assess learning progress, and I would fine-tune my instructional plans or materials. These included the following:

- written submissions
- small-group discussions
- presentations
- drafts of work
- emails
- meetings during office hours
- talk during whole-class discussions
- discussion board postings

I also shared what I paid attention to and looked for evidence of:

- conceptual understanding (or misconception)
- questions
- interaction patterns
- who talks? who doesn't?
- correct/incorrect information
- procedural understanding (or misconception)

and that deciding how to use these data required on-the-spot decision making that considered the magnitude of the problem/question/misunderstanding, what I knew about the person(s) I was responding to, and how immediately the issue needed to be addressed.

If I could see that multiple students misunderstood some procedural aspect of what we were doing, I could clarify instructions for everyone. Was it really something that needed correction, or just a different perspective or opinion? In the latter case, perhaps a later discussion of issues, or articles or position papers shared, would be more valuable than expressing disagreement on the spot. Valuing and treating with respect the person in front of me are always necessary. Having made these thought processes explicit along the way, I could refer back to them in conferences during workshop time when they were particularly relevant to the problem an individual or team was trying to solve in their learning plan.

Summative Assessment of My Candidates

In lieu of a final exam, I scheduled thirty-minute individual conferences with candidates during exam week. Ahead of that time, they submitted materials—the learning and unit plans, and final evaluation letters—that I read and annotated in preparation for the meetings. I also filled out the unit and lesson evaluation rubrics myself, and a good part of our final conferences was comparing our results and clearing up any related misunderstandings that arose from this exercise. The plans these students wrote were so good that we decided to compile a CD that included all of their plans as well as the books recommended by them in their Children's Literature wikis (explained in chapter 5). Here are the instructions they received about what they needed to submit:

1. A hard copy of your learning plan and lesson plan, with your self-assessments (UbD design standards, TEAM planning rubric) attached. In detail:
   • learning plan for entire unit, with UbD design standards checklist on top, filled out by you
   • one day's lesson plan, with TEAM planning rubric on top, filled out by you
2. A hard copy of your final evaluation letter, in which you assign yourself a grade for our Friday portion of 422, and tell me how you determined it. Be sure that you include discussion of the following:
   • your learning plan, and the process of constructing it
   • your development in understanding our four "big questions"
     1. Who are my students?
     2. What do I want them to learn?
     3. What would count as a good job of learning?
     4. How do I organize resources to accomplish #2 and #3 above?
3. An electronic copy of your learning plan, in Word (.doc or .docx) format, as an attachment to Colleen's email (cgilrane@utk.edu). When I have them all, and you've all had an opportunity to revise/edit as needed (following my feedback), I'll compile them all on CDs for all of us to keep. I'll give you your CD at your final evaluation conference.

Grades for the Friday Portion of ELED 422

Classes with multiple instructors must always wrestle with how to manage grading, and for ELED 422 it is particularly complex, as three different cohorts shared the same three instructors for the content-focused Mondays (five weeks each) while they each had their own instructor for the Friday portion. The system we settled on allowed each of the Monday instructors 100 points, and the Friday instructor 200 points, so that there were a total of 500 points available for the entire course. As you read above, for my Friday section, I asked the candidates to assign themselves the points and tell me how they determined the number.

I do this in methods courses for two different, but important, reasons. One is that teachers wield enormous power in their authority over grading;

indeed, in households all over America there is stress on report card day! Our candidates have so far only experienced this as students, and before they begin doing it as teachers, I want them to go through *the experience of turning learning into a number or letter*. It should be no surprise, if you've read this far, to learn that I believe such an activity is ridiculous—yet not one we should undertake lightly. I tell my students that I do not wish to cause anyone pain, but I know many of them will wrestle with this and I believe that's a good thing. They are less likely, I think, to be cavalier in their grading of children having done so.

Final evaluation conferences are often fruitful sites of discussion about what should count toward a grade, or what an "A" or a "B" on a transcript should stand for, based on what is written in these letters about the process for determining the grade. After twenty-two years of engaging in this process, it continues to be the case that when I disagree with my students about their grades, I usually believe they have been too hard on themselves. While many skeptics over the years have expressed that they believe my system invites students not to take my courses seriously, the data demonstrate that this is not true. In this case, Friday points assigned were comparatively lower (when scaled) to the points earned in Monday classes, and many students over the years have expressed sentiments similar to these from Claire L., for whom ELED 422 was her third class with me:

> The first time that I had to assign myself a grade, I thought that it was really weird and I didn't like it. However, now that I've done it a couple of times, I believe that being in charge of my own grade makes me work even harder. I don't want to cheat myself by setting the bar too low, yet I still want to make an A. I think that this drives me to work even harder to do my best because I know that I'm the one who ultimately has to be comfortable with the grade I give myself.

Quality control is built into the system in the form of the reflections that must be written about the various course engagements—one simply cannot write them if one was not there, and prepared, and engaged. I tell my students that I will submit the grade they propose if the letter is complete, and I will return it to them to revise and resubmit if it is not. The very small number of times over the years (four, I believe) that it was necessary, appropriately low grades were submitted by students.

The second reason I set up this system is to attempt to ameliorate the power differential that might otherwise preclude candidates from viewing me as a colleague, albeit one with more experience than they have! While I do, of course, have responsibilities for a course that are different from theirs, I don't want them filtering every question they might ask, or opinion they might express, or decision they might make by wondering how or if it will affect their grade. I don't want to prepare teachers who are other-directed (Lanier & Little, 1986) or who prefer carrying out the goals and plans of others (Shannon, 1989, 1990) to making decisions themselves. If my classes are to be places that help them develop dispositions as informed decision makers, I must do what I can to make the environment hospitable for that, and this grading scheme has that aim.

Best of all, the projects and/or portfolios are engaging to review, the letters are generally much more interesting to read than final exams would be, and the feedback we get about the depth and durability of student learning is generally positive. A variety of indicators—performance on Praxis exams, principals who want to hire our candidates based on previous experiences, instructors of subsequent courses or internships relating how prepared candidates were in the areas engaged in the course—point toward the benefit of engaged participation in authentic activities as a valid form of assessment (Hickey & Zuiker, 2005; Jurow et al., 2012). Candidates themselves notice that the system allows them to be more focused on learning, as expressed by Cameron:

> Unlike many other courses I have taken, this class was not about just learning things and memorizing the material for a test and soon forgetting much of what I had learned. . . . I was able to set aside the stress I would have had about memorizing facts for tests, which made me able to focus on the material we were discussing and actually figure out how to use it in a classroom. Taking the time to construct my learning plan step by step and only focusing on one at a time has helped me to better understand the components of a lesson. Before taking this course, writing a lesson plan on my own seemed terrifying and almost impossible.

FRIDAY CLASS SESSIONS DEVOTED TO ASSESSMENT AS A STAND-ALONE TOPIC

We spent two of our Friday mornings dealing with the topic of assessment itself. First, we talked about performance assessments and the role they might play as authentic targets toward which instruction could be directed. Then, we looked at formative assessments as tools to inform the journey. I describe each below and include the readings we happened to use, simply as examples to consider as you select your own readings informed by the needs and plans of your own candidates.

Performance Assessment

In preparation for this class session, I asked candidates to read one article in common, "Put Understanding First" (Wiggins & McTighe, 2008), and to choose one other from seven I made available on Blackboard. While the article specifically addresses teaching and learning in the high school, its principles are relevant to schools at all levels. I believed its focus on older students would capitalize on the candidates' recent experiences as high school and college students themselves, and that it could serve as a good advance organizer for our discussion of authentic assessment. This paragraph serves as a good summary of the problem:

> Out-of-context learning of skills is arguably one of the greatest weaknesses of the secondary curriculum—the natural outgrowth of marching through the textbook instead of teaching with meaning and transfer in mind. Schools too often teach and test mathematics, writing, and world language skills in isolation rather than in the context of authentic demands requiring thoughtful application. If we don't give students sufficient ongoing opportunities to puzzle over genuine problems, make meaning of their learning, and apply content in various contexts, then long-term retention and effective performance are unlikely, and high schools will have failed to achieve their purpose. (Wiggins & McTighe, 2008, p. 37)

I also asked the candidates to

> look over the Performance Assessment section of your *Understanding by Design PD Workbook*, and be ready to work in groups using pp. 157–69 to develop ideas for performance assessments in the content-area/grade-level standards you worked with last week.

When they arrived in class Friday morning, the charts they had created of "advice for teaching [content] at [grade level]" (described in chapter 3) were posted on the walls. After a whole-class meeting in which we discussed the articles and addressed questions or concerns raised, the candidates reformed into their small groups and began to generate ideas for authentic performance assessments in their targeted areas. Supports were available in several of the articles that were posted, as well as in the highlighted workbook pages that included examples and a variety of possible procedures and graphic organizers to think through this aspect of learning design. I, of course, circulated among the groups, listening, conferring, and collecting formative assessment data.

These are the readings we used to inform our conversation about performance assessment:

Brown, K. (2009). Questions for the 21st-century learner. *Knowledge Quest, 38* (1), 24–29.
Emberger, M. (2006). Helping teachers think like "assessors." *Principal, 85* (4), 38–40.

Levy, S. (2000). Building a culture where high quality counts. In A. L. Costa & B. Kallick (Eds.), *Assessing and reporting on the habits of mind* (pp. 84–105). Alexandria, VA: Association for Supervision and Curriculum Development.

McTighe, J., & O'Connor, K. (2005). Seven practices for effective learning. *Educational Leadership, 63* (3), 10–17.

McTighe, J., Seif, E., & Wiggins, G. (2004). You can teach for meaning. *Educational Leadership, 62*, 26–30.

McTighe, J., & Wiggins, G. (2004). *Understanding by design professional development workbook.* Alexandria, VA: Association for Supervision and Curriculum Development.

Richardson, J. (2008). Evidence of learning: A conversation with Jay McTighe. *Principal Leadership, 9* (1), 30–34.

Wiggins, G. (2006). Healthier testing made easy: The idea of authentic assessment. http://www.edutopia.org.

Wiggins, G., & McTighe, J. (2008). Put understanding first. *Educational Leadership, 65* (8), 36–41.

Formative Assessment

Some of the most useful work in formative assessment—at least based on years of feedback from students of mine at all levels—is that being done by Doug Fisher and Nancy Frey at San Diego State University (Fisher & Frey, 2007, 2009). Candidates especially appreciate their article in *The Reading Teacher* (Frey & Fisher, 2010) identifying crucial moves in teacher talk to scaffold children's learning and sharing a "decision making tree" that they developed to describe *how* teachers know *what* to say to children *when*. After a conversation in which I shared this feedback with him, Doug was gracious enough to send me two versions of a transcript from their research data informing this work: one plain, and one color-coded to identify the different purposes of the teacher's talk.

Similar to our routine in previous sessions, in preparation for this class meeting I asked candidates to read one piece in common (a Fisher and Frey piece) and to read a second piece of their choice; the rest of the pieces varied in the content and levels for which they provided examples, but all focused on the idea of formative assessment as a tool to support ongoing learning and that it needed to serve the purpose of giving feedback to learners about how they were doing rather than to "count" as a grade or other summative evaluation. Having posted the uncoded transcript on Blackboard, I asked the candidates to do the following:

> Download the guided instruction conversation transcript, and read it, paying careful attention to the teacher's talk. See if you can determine when the teacher is

- using robust questions to check for understanding
- prompting for knowledge the student has
- cueing to shift the student's focus of attention

Bring your coded copy to class, and we will all share and discuss our interpretations.

We had a lively discussion of this during our class meeting, following an introductory conversation in which candidates had opportunities to raise issues and questions from the readings. For each teacher move in the transcript, candidates shared their ideas about the role that talk was playing in supporting the children's understanding; once we had reached a consensus, I shared the one with Doug's and Nancy's coding. I asked candidates if they could recall my ever using talk in these ways when I interacted with them in their small-group work. Facial expressions were particularly interesting to watch in response, as even those who could not share specifics seemed to have "A-ha!" moments recognizing that this phenomenon had occurred.

These are the readings we used to inform our conversation about formative assessment:

Brown, S. (2004–2005). Assessment for learning. *Learning and Teaching in Higher Education, 1*, 81–89.

Fisher, D., & Frey, N. (2007). Using questions to check for understanding. In D. Fisher & N. Frey, *Checking for understanding: Formative assessment techniques for your classroom* (pp. 36–56). Alexandria, VA: Association for Supervision and Curriculum Development.

Fisher, D., & Frey, N. (2009). Feed up, back, forward. *Educational Leadership, 67* (3), 20–25.

Frey, N., & Fisher, D. (2010). Identifying instructional moves during guided learning. *Reading Teacher, 64* (2), 84–95.

Ginsburg, H. P. (2009). The challenge of formative assessment in mathematics education: Children's minds, teachers' minds. *Human Development, 52*, 109–28.

Wiggins, G. (2004). Assessment as feedback. *New Horizons for Learning Online Journal.* http://www.nysaae.org/.

DESIGNING ASSESSMENTS FOR LEARNING PLANS

As in all areas, the most productive and challenging work with respect to assessment took place when the candidates were designing their own learning plans. Candidates had UbD materials available to help them think, building on the rehearsal they had done in our Friday class session on performance assessment, and the syllabus directed their attention to those sections dealing with generating assessment ideas, designing assessment tasks, and developing scoring criteria. Many of my most intense conferences with candidates took place during this stage of their design, such as the one described in chapter 1 with Nancy and her partner about clarifying the place of work habits—and their evaluation—when designing assessments that are learning focused. Candidates acknowledged the challenges and rewards of this process, as Emily wrote, *I had to fight the tendency to not think of all the "fun" and creative activities I could do before I wrote my assessment.* Christine went into detail about how much work this was:

> It was very difficult for me to try to think about what I wanted my students to accomplish rather than what activity I wanted them to do. I found it particularly challenging to think about stage 2: evidence. I really had no clue how to design something for them to accomplish before them actually doing it. It makes complete sense to design curriculum in this manner, but it seems to take double the amount of work, which is what I believe our students need. They need to know that we value them and also put in just the amount of work that they do.

WHAT WOULD COUNT AS EVIDENCE: WHAT DID CANDIDATES LEARN?

The candidates' learning plans demonstrated that, at least in this one example, they were able to move beyond typical school assessments and be thoughtful about assessing to support learning, rather than just for a score or grade. In their final evaluation letters, their reflections indicated that this disposition was more durable, and that in their own teaching they might continue to move beyond surface-level assessments, turn a critical lens on typical procedures, and capitalize on their own student experiences when they assess their children.

Assessment Beyond Worksheets and Tests

In their final evaluation letters, most candidates reflected that to some extent they recognized the necessity not to settle for tests and worksheets as indicators of their children's learning. Allie talks about how her own thinking shifted:

> When I was in elementary school, I remember having lots of worksheets and tests that would count towards my grade. Therefore, when we started studying the third "big question," what could I count as a good job of learning, it made me realize there are so many other ways to assess students without giving them tests and worksheets. I think using formative assessments would be more ben-

eficial because you can determine each individual's progress throughout the unit instead of just at the end. Also, I found it really interesting to learn about all the ways to assess students without using worksheets and paper and pencil tests. I plan to have conferences with my students to determine how much they are learning and if they are having any difficulties. I also hope to have choices for my students, like book reports, book talks, drawing pictures, writing in journals, and allowing them to be creative. I think students learn even more when they are able to show what they have learned in different ways. What works with one student might not always work with another. Therefore, I want to offer choice for my students and also make assessments different than paper and pencil tests and worksheets.

VB expressed similar ideas, and referred to specific assessment tasks that she had incorporated into her learning plan:

"What would count as a good job of learning?" At first I would have been the typical "teach-to-the-test" type of teacher. A good job of learning means they can pass the test is what my answer would have been. However, I have now realized that there may be some kids that will never pass a test, whether it is standardized or not, if teachers do not quit using worksheets and worksheet types of tests. My math lesson that I created helped me to get a little bit of experience creating an assessment that was not in that style. I made my assessment a performance assessment where there are students that are customers and students that are bankers. They would pretend to be in a store but they would be meeting the third grade standards of counting coins up to $5 and giving change within $1. I have now realized that a good job of learning means that students can apply the information you have been teaching in one way or another.

Bringing a Critical Lens to Current Practice

Some candidates' reflections moved beyond awareness of additional possibilities to the importance of evaluating and critiquing current practices. Kelly had this to say:

Another question to consider is "What would count as a good job of learning?" This is where we need to look at our activities and our assessments. If a student can simply repeat back a piece of information, does that mean he/she actually understands it? We need to be critical of our activities and assessments and make sure they actually enhance and represent the child's full understanding.

Adalee reflected on the difference between lessons she observed in person and those in Steven Levy's classroom:

If I have learned one thing while being in the education program at UT, it would be that standardized tests do not give students a way to really show what they know. There will always be students who are good at tests in general, and there will be those who get test anxiety. Furthermore, being able to recognize facts does not demonstrate deep understanding.

Backwards planning is very important in the process of deciding how to assess students. Students need to know where they are headed and what they will be expected to do with the information that is presented to them.

Authentic assessments are valuable. Many times students complain that they will not use what they are learning in real life. By allowing students to engage in a real world task with what they are learning, they will understand the importance of what they are being taught. A great example of this is Steven Levy's classroom. Instead of just learning about area and perimeter on paper, they were using the skills to actually build something! This semester I got to observe in a 4th grade classroom. The only experiences they had with area and perimeter were on worksheets. I could only think about how much more students would understand if they could have a hands-on, authentic task.

Bringing Student Experiences to Bear on Designing Assessments as Teachers

Candidates often reflect on how initially disconcerting—yet eventually powerful—it is not to be focused on grades and points in our class, such as Cameron's reflection above, and these thoughts shared by Maggie:

> I had a profound revelation during the semester: If grades do not exist, then artificial perfection does not exist. With that pressure off my shoulders, I was able to put aside my drive to achieve a perfect score and simply focus on learning.

Most of them eventually take the next step and bring that awareness to their teaching and assessing of children. For some, it happens after the course is finished, when they've had more time to digest it; for others, it happens earlier, such as in this reflection by Alice:

> When I think about the question, "What would count as a good job of learning," I definitely reflect on this class and all that I have learned from you. I have never had a professor be so passionate about a way of teaching. I really liked the fact that we were presented a new and effective way of teaching that does not involve a lecture style classroom. It really opened my eyes to new avenues by being able to watch Levy's videos and hearing your insight on teaching. I was brought up on the "grade" system of knowing if a student did a good job of an activity, but now I have altered my thought process of how to teach and what to consider a good job of learning. I will make sure I am consistently using formative assessments to understand a student's progress throughout the school year and more specifically throughout the lesson.

Chapter Five

Question #4: How Do I Get There?

Eight weeks into the semester, we finally arrived at the topic most of the candidates would have thought was the starting place of planning. Having now thoroughly explored questions #1 through #3, we began to talk about the role of instructional "activities," selecting from all that is available the materials, activities/engagements, personnel, instructional strategies, time, space, and environmental resources that would support their own students' learning for deep understanding. We devoted three Friday mornings to this as a stand-alone topic before diving into the meat of designing learning plans itself: one each for materials, personnel and instructional strategies, and time/space/environment.

SELECTING INSTRUCTIONAL MATERIALS

Knowing that five weeks of work actually selecting materials to accomplish learning goals was on the horizon, and knowing that the candidates were immersed in learning about appropriate math, science, and social studies materials in their Monday classes, I determined that one week was enough to spend on materials, and that we would use that week to talk about selections of children's literature. I hoped that the ways I asked candidates to think about this would transfer to their eventual selection of all materials: What content is this related to? Why is it worth my time? How will I use it? Will my children relate to it?

As you have no doubt predicted, there was one article we read in common, and others that candidates could select, depending on what particular aspect of using children's books was most compelling for them at the time—a content area, perhaps? or multicultural issues? I then wanted them to use what they'd read to inform selections of children's books to share with the rest of us. Here's the assignment as it appeared in the syllabus:

Since you are focusing on appropriate materials for science, social studies, and math on Mondays, we will spend time with books here.

Read the Gilrane piece, and one other article of your choice. Then, find at least three children's books that would be worth using in your classroom.

Go to the wiki setup for this class session, and add a page sharing your books with the rest of us. Be sure to include at least

- complete bibliographic information
- a brief synopsis of the book
- the content standards it is related to
- the criteria you used to select it (how did you decide it is worth your time?)
- any ideas you have for using it

Feel free to add anything else (links, reviews, graphics, etc.) that will help us know enough about your books to decide if we want to find copies ourselves!

Please post to the wiki by [date] at 8:00 a.m., and bring your books to class on Friday, [date].

The class session during which books were shared was one of the candidates' favorites, and the wikis eventually became a resource document on the CD with the learning plans. Following are the readings we used to inform our work; no doubt, as newer excellent materials become available, those will be more useful. This list is shared simply as an example of the variety that is available when teachers seek to find books that are appropriate for different content goals.

Gilrane, C. P. (2009). So many books—how do I choose? In D. A. Wooten & B. E. Cullinan, (Eds.), *Children's literature in the reading program: An invitation to read* (pp. 130–40). Newark, DE: International Reading Association.

Jones, T. (2012). Combining geocaching and children's literature. *Journal of Studies in Education, 2* (1), 30–38.

Kinniburgh, L. H., & Byrd, K. (2008). Ten black dots and September 11: Integrating social studies and mathematics through children's literature. *The Social Studies, 99*, 33–36.

Lintner, T. (2010). Using children's literature to promote critical geographic awareness in elementary classrooms. *The Social Studies, 101*, 17–24.

McKnight, D. M. (2010). Overcoming "ecophobia": Fostering environmental empathy through narrative in children's science literature. *Frontiers in Ecology and the Environment, 8* (6), 10–15.

Palmer, J., & Burroughs, S. (2002). Integrating children's literature and song into the social studies. *The Social Studies, 93* (2), 73–78.

Rearden, K. T., & Broemmel, A. D. (2008). Beyond the talking groundhogs: Trends in science trade books. *Journal of Elementary Science Education, 20* (2), 39–49.

Sackes, M., Trundle, K. C., & Flevares, L. M. (2009). Using children's literature to teach standard-based science concepts in early years. *Early Childhood Education Journal, 36*, 415–22.

Shatzer, J. (2008). Picture book power: Connecting children's literature and mathematics. *Reading Teacher, 61*, 649–53.

Souto-Manning, M. (2009). Negotiating culturally responsive pedagogy through multicultural children's literature: Towards critical democratic literacy practices in a first grade classroom. *Journal of Early Childhood Literacy, 9* (1), 50–74.

Ward, R. A. (2005). Using children's literature to inspire K–8 preservice teachers' future mathematics pedagogy. *The Reading Teacher, 59*, 132–43.

SELECTING PERSONNEL RESOURCES AND INSTRUCTIONAL STRATEGIES

I was fortunate (and still am) to be a member of a teacher research group whose members included a coteaching coach from the district in which our interns would be placed. Coteaching in this specific context referred to

> the deployment of a general education teacher and a special education teacher to work with a class of diverse students. Both educators assume full responsibility for the education of all students in the classroom, including planning, presentation, classroom management, and evaluation. (Gately, 2005, p. 36)

In a more generic context, it can mean "teaching at another teacher's elbow and taking shared responsibility for all parts of lessons" (Roth & Tobin, 2004, p. 161), whether specifically addressing inclusion and special education or not. In fact, coteaching is the best term to describe what our interns and their mentors do during the full-year graduate internship, and it supports the mutual growth and development of both teachers. At its best, coteaching uses a variety of teaching arrangements, including whole-class teacher led, two heterogeneous groups, two homogeneous groups, station teaching, whole class plus small group, and whole-class team teaching (Solis, Vaughn, Swanson, & McCulley, 2012, p. 504).

Our candidates encountered the term *coteaching* in their special education course in the elementary minor, and we arranged for our elementary candidates and our special education candidates to spend as much time as possible together during their preparation to encourage their collaborative work later. I was excited about the opportunity to bring my colleague and her team to visit with our class about how coteaching was lived out in the district in which they'd be interning. The coteaching coaches worked in teams of two—one with special education license and teaching experience, the other with general education—and she brought her partner as well as their supervisor to our class.

In the Friday morning session that the coteaching coaches spent with us, our candidates were able to see demonstrated a variety of the instructional strategies they'd been introduced to in other courses, as well as experience four of the six teaming arrangements listed above. The coaches used station teaching as an opportunity to get to know a bit about the candidates quickly, and posted six charts around the room, with these titles:

Accepting Attitude
Ability to Implement Activity-Based Learning
Effective Classroom Management Skills
Desire to Work Collaboratively
High Expectations
Ability to Work with Different Ability Levels

The candidates then, in six small groups, spent time at each poster discussing what its heading meant to them or made them think of, which they could record with markers. One of the charts is shown in figure 5.1; the coaches told me later how grateful they were to learn of the openness of our candidates to inclusive teaching.

There were also small groups discussing articles the coaches brought, a whole-class team-taught lecture using PowerPoint, and a whole-class teacher-led Q & A at the end of class, following the watching of a video visit to several coteaching classrooms—not only the professionally produced ones similar to what they'd seen in other classes but also locally produced ones in district classrooms. During a break, candidates were invited to write questions they had on sticky notes and attach them to the board if they did not feel comfortable asking those out loud; you can see them at the bottom of the poster in figure 5.1. The coaches addressed all of these questions, even sending me via email their responses to the ones left when time ran out in class:

Q: In using the alternative model as it was used in the video, it seemed like the large group teacher/teaching would be very distracting to the small group. Could you meet in the hallway or a different area instead, or is it best to stay in the room?

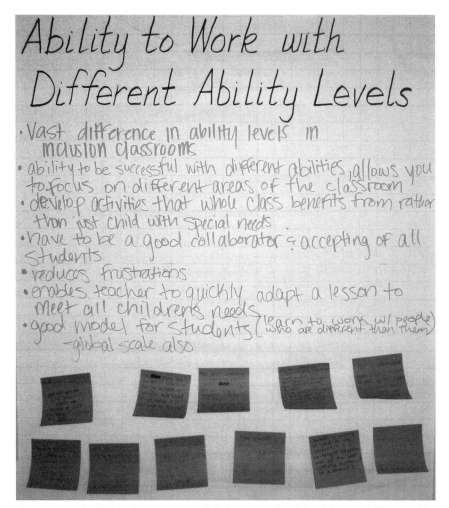

Figure 5.1. Candidates' Responses to "Ability to Work With Different Ability Levels"

A: Coteaching takes place in a shared space with shared resources. When alternate spaces are used for instruction, coteaching turns into pullout services and no longer meets the true definition of coteaching. There could be legal issues that arise from this practice as well (such as when a special educator delivers pullout services to students without IEPs or when a special educator leaves students with IEPs in the room, thus potentially violating the required amount of service time as indicated on the IEPs).

Q: The movie said to come up with different reasons as to why you pull a small group of children from the main group, yet the video continually said to pull kids who look confused, who are falling behind, etc. Clearly they are just pulling the struggling kids. How do you avoid the embarrassment for the pulled students?

A: Unfortunately the video models demonstrated the use of small groups to meet the needs of the struggling students. However, in practice teachers are using those small groups for a variety of reasons that do not necessarily target only the needs of the students facing challenges. These flexible, differentiated groupings are occurring right here in [District] Schools. Group composition should change often. One of the reasons for continually changing small-group selection criteria is to avoid potential student embarrassment.

Q: How do you keep kids from getting embarrassed when you pull them into an alternative group?

A: Please see the above response.

Other sticky note questions were answered orally, in class, and I don't have a record of the responses, but the coaches and I were all pleased with how engaged the candidates were in the conversation, and how that was reflected in the questions they asked, which included the following:

How do you go about introducing the idea/concept of coteaching to a school who doesn't do it or has never even heard of it?

How can you be sure you won't be viewed as just "the helper" if you're the SPED teacher?

How do administrators decide which two teachers to pair up for coteaching? This dynamic seems so important yet complex. What if you don't get along?

Of course, that last question was of concern to all, whether or not they'd ever be part of a formal coteaching team, as the dynamic asked about is critical to the intern/mentor teacher relationship as well. I expect that the article the coaches shared called "20 Ways to Strengthen Your Coteaching Relationship" (Stivers, 2008) was eventually consulted by all, and perhaps shared . . . and as you will read in chapter 9, interns receive coaching from Kristin in this area as well.

MAKING DECISIONS ABOUT TIME, SPACE, ENVIRONMENT, AND PULLING IT ALL TOGETHER

Finally, it was our last Friday meeting before the beginning of design workshop! What I wanted to do with this session was to provide an advance organizer for the backward-design process (Wiggins & McTighe, 2005) that we'd begin after spring break, as well as deal with whatever issues were critical for the candidates at that time. To prepare for this class, I asked them to read an introduction to the design process, and then to *choose one or more of the other pieces based on what you are most concerned about right now.* Our meeting was pretty free flowing as candidates raised issues and I or their colleagues responded. We were all ready to engage in the design process itself! The articles below are the ones that, along with candidates' concerns, informed our discussion on this day.

Brown, D. F. (2003). Urban teachers' use of culturally responsive management strategies. *Theory into Practice, 42* (4), 277–82.

Marzano, R., Pickering, D. J., & Pollock, J. E. (2001). Using the nine categories in instructional planning. In R. Marzano, D. J. Pickering, & J. E. Pollock, *Classroom instruction that works* (pp. 146–55). Alexandria, VA: Association for Supervision and Curriculum Development.

McTighe, J., & Brown, J. L. (2005). Differentiated instruction and educational standards: Is détente possible? *Theory into Practice, 44* (3), 234–44.

Page, B. (2010). 12 things teachers must know about learning. *Education Digest, 75* (8), 54–56.

Saphier, J., Haley-Speca, M. A., & Gower, R. (2008). *The skillful teacher: Building your teaching skills.* (Summary of classroom management ideas and strategies).

Wiggins, G. (1989). The futility of trying to teach everything of importance. *Educational Leadership, 47*, 44–59.

HOW DO I GET THERE: WHAT DID CANDIDATES LEARN?

The learning plans and lesson plans themselves reflected the variety of resources marshaled by our candidates to support their children, and in their final evaluation letters they all reflected on the design process itself and how well it worked for them; many of their thoughts on this have already been shared in the previous chapters addressing specific stages in the process. Christine's is an example of candidates' reflection on the process overall, and waiting so long to get to the actual learning design:

> Although I have been greatly challenged by the concept, I am slowly beginning to love and admire backwards design as a process. If I were a student in my class

I would want to know what I had to do before I was just thrown a large amount of information. When you are building a building you have an idea before you decide how you are going to build it. When you are teaching a concept it is important that you know what you want students to be able to accomplish before you give them a list of instructions.

Candidates also reflected more specifically on their thinking about resources. In the sections below, I will share reflections that represent their learning in three areas: an expanded view of resources and their selection, the importance of time and timing, and the idea of personnel as resources.

Expanded Awareness of Resources

For many of our candidates, an important learning outcome of our design process is that it does not begin with textbooks—as does so much of the schooling in their own experiences! By beginning with learning goals and aiming toward authentic performance assessments as the demonstration of learning, we put textbooks and other materials in their rightful places as resources that might be selected by a teacher if they support the children's learning. While our teaching them to think this way used to make some of them nervous—what if my school/principal/mentoring teacher won't let me do these things?—in recent years that anxiety has been lessened, as the TEAM rubric awards higher scores to lessons with more resources than textbooks! VB's reflection is one example of a candidate's expanded view of resources available for teaching:

> The last question, "organizing resources," I would have said that it means finding the worksheets and the test questions to give the students after the teacher instruction. I would have said there need to be some manipulatives just to use as an example during teaching, but I would put them away or only allow them out for certain problems. I would not have done this to be the mean teacher, but this is the way I was always taught and I had never seen any teaching in another way. Now I realize that gathering and organizing resources means so much more than just picking out your objects.

Following up on this wealth of available resources, Claire F. pointed out the importance of selecting wisely from among them:

> Lastly, I have learned how many resources there are at my disposal to promote learning, including ideas from peers/colleagues, SmartBoards, and children's books. But choosing these resources wisely is key. It is easy to get caught up in the cuteness of an activity or develop an elaborate, impressive lesson but this

might not maximize the students' learning. The focus should be on the students, and what materials I can bring in and use that will best help and teach them.

Time as a Resource

Several candidates addressed the issue of time and its scarcity, and the importance of making instructional decisions that use every minute of it to advantage. Elsie talked about the importance of making these selections later in the process than she had previously believed, to be fair to her students and make good use of their time:

> I used to ask this question first when I was thinking of planning a lesson. It is easy to run to textbooks and Pinterest when thinking of ideas for lessons. But I have learned that this needs to come last in order to be fair to my students in the future. I have also realized that when you approach the resources last, there are so many things you can do!

Kelly shared her thoughts about time in two ways, not only not wasting it but also being thoughtful about sequencing of learning experiences:

> This last question is equally important to consider. This has to do with considering the resources that help reach the goals of the last two questions. First, it's important to consider all the available resources and judge if they are worthy of the students' time. We have to decide if these resources will enhance learning or if they will be a distraction. We must be careful that we don't bring in resources that we think are fun or cute but actually have no or very little educational value. And second, we have to decide how to organize these resources and make them fit in the most logical order possible. This is important because it is necessary to build off what students already know.

Personnel as Resources

The thought of people as instructional resources was not one all of our candidates had encountered before, or considered explicitly, but our coteaching coaches and the use of community resources by Steven Levy made this one they were eager to explore. Cassie shared ideas other than coteaching as she reflected on resources:

> Coteaching is an excellent example of really utilizing another person to help with teaching, but it is certainly not the only way to use personnel as a resource. Simply talking to and getting to know fellow teachers who share your same beliefs is an excellent way to get some good ideas and advice.

As I read Adalee's reflection on inviting others into her classroom, I appreciated how careful and critical her thinking was about whom she might bring in:

> I had not thought about how other people can be used as a resource either. Not only will getting to know the community help me understand student perspectives, but I can also use people from the community in my classroom. I understand that it will be important to utilize people from different backgrounds and genders so that I will not reinforce stereotypes. I could have people who have different jobs come in and talk about the skill sets that they use. This could help students learn why some topics are important in school.

INTERLUDE:
VOICES OF CANDIDATES

Chapter Six

Hannah's Reflection

Upon entering Colleen's class as a preservice teacher, I was just becoming familiarized with the rubric jargon of high-stakes teacher evaluations such as TEAM and edTPA, as well as the new Common Core standards. At the time, I had taken a few graduate methods courses that had introduced me to the new teaching ideals. With new information and the stress I overheard from the interns and professors at the time, I was relieved when Colleen came to class and said she had a plan. Her plan was simple: teach us to teach for deep understanding. She wanted us to always begin by asking ourselves: "Who are my students?" and "What do I want them to learn?" Her plan made sense. Why would she teach us to teach according to TEAM or edTPA when the rubrics may change by the time we even find a job? Colleen believed that as our professor, it was her duty to ask herself "Who are my students?" and "What do I want them to learn?" Her students were preservice teachers wading through a sea of rubrics, and she wanted us to learn how to be teachers that teach for deep understanding regardless of the latest rubric in the shifting landscape of teacher evaluations.

Colleen charged us with creating a learning plan as our semester-long project. This was her method for teaching us, preservice teachers, how to filter through information, rubrics, and teach for enduring understanding. She presented this concept through backward design (McTighe & Thomas, 2003; Wiggins & McTighe, 2008). I spent the greatest amount of time in Stage 1 of backward design: establishing goals, establishing enduring understandings, creating essential questions, and choosing the knowledge and skills we wanted our students to be able to do. After choosing the standards and goals of my learning plan, I followed Colleen's instructions to then focus on what I wanted my students to know, understand, and be able to do. The backward

design concept helps teachers create learning plans that teach for deep understanding. This philosophy of planning is in stark contrast to simply creating
activities associated with standards or looking at a rubric and trying to make
the standards fit. Then, after distinguishing what I wanted my students to take
away from the lessons, I could ask myself: "What will count as evidence of
their learning?" This stage is where I considered what learning tasks and assessments would provide my students the opportunity to show me what they
had learned from the lesson.

This is where a teacher must get creative and know his or her students.
Maybe I will assess their learning by allowing them to create their own
products: they could show me what they have learned through digital media,
writing, oral reports, or illustrations, to name a few. Only after deciding what
counts as evidence of student learning could I choose authentic learning activities for lessons. For instance, I decided my students would show me what
they had learned about decisions and consequences (second-grade Social
Studies standard) by focusing on the book *The Lorax* by Dr. Seuss. I decided
to first have the students debate, as Once-lers and Loraxes, the consequences
of cutting down the Truffula trees. After a whole-class debate, I planned to
ask students to write an alternate conclusion to *The Lorax*. At the end of the
story, the reader is left with the decision of what to do with the final tree
seedling. Their written alternate conclusions of what to do with the final tree
seedling would show me the extent of what they had learned—that they can
make a decision and identify the potential consequences of that decision,
good or bad. This assessment would inform my instruction and also show me
how deep their understanding went, much more so than a multiple-choice test
related to the social studies curriculum. I feel that the philosophy of backward
design planning prompts the teacher to plan for more meaningful learning
tasks and assessments. In turn, students are stretched in their thinking and
gain a deeper and more transferable understanding of the content taught.

TRANSITIONING TO INTERNSHIP

After gaining a teaching foundation in Colleen's preservice class, I entered
graduate school and became a full-time teaching intern under Dr. Rearden's
supervision. My deep-rooted understandings about how to teach for deep understanding versus a rubric (from Colleen's class) continued with me through
my internship as I began planning real lessons for "real" students for the first
time. Colleen and Dr. Rearden's classes and philosophies helped me to realize the difficulty in slowing down and planning for enduring understanding.
It is easy to think of fun activities for a lesson, but are they meaningful? Are

the students taking something away? What I learned from my professors was exceedingly constructive to my teaching during my internship year in a second-grade classroom.

During the internship, Dr. Rearden saw me through my completion of edTPA and four of my formal TEAM evaluations. She continued, however, to teach us about teaching for enduring understanding in our graduate classes. She let that knowledge seep into edTPA and teacher evaluations. When I say she "saw me through" the process, I really mean just that: Dr. Rearden did not teach me, or my cohort, edTPA or TEAM; she taught us how to teach. Because of that, I cannot express how prepared I had felt and had been for those rubrics and assessments. I never doubted that I planned good lessons for edTPA or evaluations, because I knew I focused on good teaching and not the rubrics. Good teaching is good teaching. It will shine through any rubrics or assessment.

Both Colleen as a professor and Dr. Rearden as my professor and intern advisor were vital in my preparedness for the new teaching ideals, high-stakes evaluations, and licensure requirements. During my internship I did exceptionally well on evaluations because of my teaching program's viewpoint on how to prepare teacher candidates. I passed edTPA (along with the rest of my entire cohort), and I scored "At Expectations" or "Above Expectations" on all of my formal TEAM evaluations. Colleen and Dr. Rearden taught me to know my students, meet their needs, and not to *worry* about the rubrics, but to translate what I was doing into rubric language, *after* I'd thought through these important issues.

FIRST-YEAR TEACHING AFTER INTERNSHIP

Now that I am a first-year teacher, you may be asking yourself; "How did all of this 'teaching for deep understanding' play out in the real world?" Stepping foot into my classroom for the first time, meeting my students, and realizing that I have to meet their needs all on my own—without the support of my professors and program—was a tad daunting. But as quickly as I could think I may not be able to do it, I realized even quicker how completely and utterly prepared I was. Without missing a beat, I jumped in, asking myself, "Who are my students?" and "What do I want them to learn?" My students are fourth-graders coming from high-poverty backgrounds who need support and solid academic instruction. I had to find out their interests, meet them on their level (most of which were below level), and help them to master the Common Core standards. Moreover, I realized that my salary and bonuses are now tied to my high-stakes TEAM evaluations and how well my students master lesson objectives, and it had never been more "real." My teacher preparation program had never been more decisive.

Teaching Science: Erosion Unit

In order to meet my students' needs and provide solid academic instruction in my classroom, I thought to myself that I must present the content in a meaningful way to my students. This gets at the heart of "Who are my students?" and "What do I want them to learn?"—I must ask myself, "What interests them? What relates to their community and neighborhood? What will instill a sense of inquiry in my specific students?" As a fourth-grade teacher, I was assigned to teach science to all of the fourth-graders in my school. One of our initial topics was erosion; the state standards wanted students to understand the types of erosion, what causes erosion, and how can humans solve erosion problems. My program had taught me to present content relevant to the students and not to rely on basals, teacher editions, or textbooks for support. With a science textbook outdated by over a decade, I was quick to realize that I would be teaching science completely on my own. Luckily, I had taken graduate-level content-specific courses that prepared me in the rich content of elementary math, English/language arts, social studies, and science. Again, I was feeling a tad insecure about whether I could teach a year's worth of fourth-grade science with no curriculum material supports, but I was up for the challenge, and I trusted (more than ever) my education and program.

After analyzing the standards myself and familiarizing myself with the content on erosion I needed to present, I was then faced with the challenge of how to make the erosion content interesting and relevant to my inner-city students. My students do not live on the beach, near the Grand Canyon, or near a glacier, which are typical examples used when teaching erosion at the elementary level. Relying on what I had learned in my program to make learning meaningful for my students, I thought, "What better place to start than right here in our own environment: the school." I began the unit by taking the fourth-graders outside with their science notebooks to collect observations of erosion around our very own school. The students were shocked to find water erosion where our gutters rushed out on the grass, and erosion by cars on our pavement in the pickup line, and erosion by humans where we line up every day to leave the playground. The sites of erosion my students started to find spurred the inquiry I needed in my students to fuel our unit of study. By the end of our guided exploration, my students had more questions than I had ever heard them ask.

We then categorized the types of erosion they found around the school, and I was then able to teach about the types of erosion and to provide rich content for what they had seen; but rather than me front-loading their experience, the note taking was much more meaningful because it was relevant to their own discoveries. This is a critical aspect of what I have called "good teaching"—providing opportunities for students to explore and make meaning of the world around them to set a context for their learning. After we mastered the standard of types of erosion through exploration, discovery, and instruction, we were then able to move on to the standard regarding humans solving erosion problems.

To motivate my students' learning about solving erosion problems, we researched occupations and people that deal with erosion on a daily basis. Many of my students were able to make contact with such experts and hear more about erosion problems all around our community and our state as a whole. I provided my students with opportunities to work collaboratively with one another to share ideas on solving the erosion problems around our school. Groups of students began to research materials, solutions, and outcomes to different types of erosion relevant to the problems we looked at around our school. Their imaginations started to run away with them, and there was no holding them back at this point. I think this is a goal every teacher has—for students to be agents of their own learning and to be captivated by finding out more information. This type of teaching and student learning will shine through any assessment.

Our erosion unit culminated with our school science fair, where my students were able to present pictures, video, and models of their erosion solutions for types of erosion around our school. Over the course of the unit, they were able to identify which type of erosion erodes different soil types the most by creating experiments on their own and collecting scientific data over the course of a month. This unit was truly a phenomenal experience to be a part of, and reflecting back I think about how dull our learning about erosion could have been if I had simply relied on a textbook or other curriculum materials. Students' driving their own learning is priceless, and the academic gains are exponential. I firmly believe that students must construct meaning of their learning if they are to learn anything at all. I came to this belief because of my program—it is how I was taught to teach—but more so because I have seen firsthand how much more learning takes place when I teach for deep understanding. The erosion unit was not created according to any rubric; however, it nonetheless met the rubric criteria for solid teaching because it focused on teaching for enduring understanding.

Teaching Math: Problems with Missing or Extra Information

Similarly, I have seen the same results in other subject areas. Science naturally lends itself to inquiry-based learning, but I have found that all subject areas must be taught with an inquiry, project-based approach. Good teaching must reap the most academic benefits while keeping children engaged and excited about learning. I was taught in my program to teach for deep under-standing, and this type of teaching reaps the most academic benefits for my students and, subsequently, my professional evaluations. For example, I had an unannounced evaluation on instruction and planning by my principal in math one day this year. Practically speaking, if I had followed the curriculum in the teacher's edition on how to teach my students "problem solving with missing and extra information," I would have scored terribly. The curriculum includes a video, then a practice worksheet, then an independent quiz at the end. Instead, I took the topic of that day as a guide, and thought about the question, "What will count as evidence of my students' learning?" This ques-tion guides the learning activities when planning. I thought that if my students could *create* their own word problems that contained either extra or missing information, *that* would show me that they had learned the concept. I did not need them to do worksheets solving missing and extra information math problems. What I needed from them was to think abstractly, as in, "What information can they pluck from or add to a word problem to heighten it to the level of either not being able to be solved or have too much information?"

My students worked with chart paper and markers collaboratively, creating first a real-word problem, and then deciding whether to take out key informa-tion or instead add extra information to essentially "trick" their classmates. Using a word like *trick* motivated my students—it was that edge I needed to fuel their learning. After creating their own problems, we hung the charts around the room, and the students did a silent "museum walk" with their math journals to solve one another's problems and to identify them as either missing or extra information problems. Again, in this lesson my students were able to show me their learning in multiple ways, I taught and provided opportunities for multiple types of thinking, my students worked in a variety of group and individual settings, and my students mastered the lesson objec-tive. These are just a handful of the indicators on the TEAM rubric on which I scored at a 3 or a 4 level. My students learned more because I taught for deep understanding, and I also benefitted from scoring "above expectations" on my own professional evaluation. This is because good teaching is good teaching, and it will be evident in any assessment or rubric.

FINAL REFLECTIONS

Luckily, my program prepared me to flourish in my first teaching. Not my first year teaching with Common Core, not my first year teaching under TEAM, and not because I completed edTPA, but because they taught me that *good teaching is good teaching.* My professors focused on teaching us to teach for deep understanding—despite the distracting focus on rubrics—and prepared me better than I realized. I have been successful in my first year of teaching and feel that I am meeting my students' needs and stretching their thinking on a daily basis. I have scored "At Expectations" and "Above Expectations" on my formal, high-stakes teacher evaluations. More importantly, I am prepared for any new state or national standards, expectations, or new teacher evaluation system. If I had been trained in my teacher preparation program solely for edTPA, for TEAM rubrics, or for the Common Core standards, I would not know how to teach. Let me reiterate: I would not know where to begin to plan a lesson that focuses on deep understanding or meets the criteria of "Above Expectations" on the rubrics. Because of my program's focus on teaching for deep understanding, I can overlay any assessment rubric, and it is simply frosting on the cake—it enhances my lessons.

Not only does this philosophy of teaching for deep understanding lead to more meaningful lessons, but I have found that by asking myself what will count as evidence of student learning, I create learning activities and assessments that are subsequently and genuinely aligned with TEAM rubrics. I believe that edTPA and TEAM rubrics have good intentions for raising the standard of teaching in schools today. To score well, a teacher must teach authentic lessons with creative assessments that allow all students the opportunity to succeed. I have learned, however, that many teachers feel unprepared to teach a lesson that will score well. Many teachers use the rubric as a checklist and have not been equipped with the skills to step back and look at the broader picture: Who are my students? What do I want them to learn? What will count as evidence of their learning? If the rubric is treated like a checklist, a lesson will collapse; when one teaches for deep understanding, the lesson thrives. Thanks to my professors' foresight about their own students, I am able to teach for deep understanding instead of teaching according to rubrics, and *still* exceed the rubric criteria for good teaching. Moreover, my students have flourished, and I am able to better meet their needs on a daily basis, which is every teacher's goal at the end of the day.

Chapter Seven

Jessica's Reflection

Educators, and those who evaluate them, should view assessments as more than a metric of their own success. In a teach-to-the-test environment, we as educators must maintain a commitment that every paper, assignment, and quiz along the way is a method of informing our instruction. I have learned that if we lose track of whom our students are when focusing on their test scores, we lose the ability to help them understand. This applies to all levels and all classrooms, but especially in special education it is imperative to know your students in order to cultivate the skills of each child. The Understanding by Design (UbD) framework (McTighe & Wiggins, 2004; Wiggins & McTighe, 2005) provided me a step-by-step process that encourages deep understanding that will stay with a student, instead of information they learn once—and forget. It is essential in the realm of education for your students to gain a real grasp of material that stretches beyond what the test requires. As a teacher, the things more daunting than the infamous test itself are the *changes that can occur without warning*, leaving your students wholly unprepared. As an intern in my school system, I set out to help my future students learn regardless of how they will be assessed by those outside my classroom. I found it was far more challenging than I had ever anticipated.

"UNDERSTANDING" ACROSS DIFFERING TEACHING CONTEXTS

As a special education teacher, I have had teaching experience in three different forms. The first is the hypothetical that all students in education are faced with when they think about the classroom they hope to have in the future. The second was practicum placements where I was in the classroom for four to nine weeks observing the teacher and assisting in teaching. The third, and most enlightening, was an internship year where I spent the first seven months of the school year in a Comprehensive Development Classroom for students in kindergarten to fifth grade. After this I spent six weeks in a high school resource classroom teaching English and world history, then another six weeks in a fourth-grade classroom. Throughout each stage of becoming a teacher, it was important to me that I strived for understanding. For the purposes of this chapter, I am defining that understanding as *lasting information to the student*. I've found this definition is versatile enough to apply to many of the levels I have had experience in because it tends toward generalization of material. I have found that in addition to asking myself who my students are, what I want them to learn, how I will gauge their progress, and how they will obtain the information, it is equally important to ask myself *where my students are going and what they need to know in order to get there.* This question ties all my planning back to the IEP goals and objectives of my students.

While students in our teacher education program's spring block, a colleague and I wrote a unit plan for a fourth-grade history class. When I came into the class, I had no idea how to develop a lesson plan, let alone one that would develop deep and lasting understanding in my diverse future class. Regardless, we set out to write a unit about colonization and settlement in the New World. When I came out of the class, I had the tools to face the prescribed lesson plan template fearlessly—resulting in a lesson plan about teaching inference making in a fourth-grade resource group, and a geometry lesson in a self-contained high school class, during my practicum placements the following year.

However, things changed as I entered my internship. Suddenly I was seeing these students from the very beginning to nearing the end and their progress became evident to me in a way I had not seen before. I was now seeing the full scope of the theories I had learned in school and implemented in my practicum. I realized something about the questions I had been taught to ask myself, especially the one I had focused on the most. I had believed that I simply combine observations of students' classroom work and the information in their IEPs in order to know my students. As I went into my internship, I realized the amount of collaboration necessary for a special educator to know her students. I have found that oftentimes the student's general education teacher or special areas teacher will see student behavior or progress that doesn't present itself in the special education classroom.

Using Knowledge of Students to Set Goals and Evaluate Learning

In school, I had been provided with the essential questions to ask myself as a teacher, the school system's prescribed lesson plan template, and the UbD system to know the steps to take before filling in the boxes of the final plan. When I entered my internship, I learned how to shape those tools to fit the classroom I was in and the student needs I was meeting.

Setting Learning Goals

To begin, we focused on the desired results of the lesson. This consistently is the largest hurdle for me, and initially the most confusing, as I was at a loss as to what exactly was asked of me. Being so used to the standards and IEP objectives as the basis for every move, it was difficult for me take a step back and think of the big picture that incorporates both those and the student. In order to find and break down the big ideas into enduring understanding, essential questions, and the knowledge and skills students will gain, you have to think about not only *what* but *why* you are teaching. This step is crucial because it not only focuses your lesson but also pushes beyond the standards. This step also encourages you to consider how the knowledge you are imparting is practical for your students.

This practicality is what pushed me to ask myself where my students were going and what I needed to do to help them get there. Students are not isolated events in our classroom, and it is important to ask ourselves as their educators about transitions and plans that will help the student achieve their long- and short-term goals. To do this, you must provide the skill set necessary to complete the task and what practical, transferable skills the students will acquire through it.

Establishing this skill set is additionally vital in Special Education because students may be at drastically different levels. This is what I learned in my year of internship. Previously, I had known that my students were at varying levels, but I hadn't considered how that affects moving from one unit or one lesson to the next. In my practicum, I taught making inferences and inquired about the student's present levels for skills such as reading comprehension and vocabulary suited for the text, and found not all of my students had those skills. To meet the diverse needs of the group, I used a wordless picture book, which helped to focus the lesson on the task at hand. Later, I found that this challenge is not always easily overcome. In my internship I taught a group of second- and third-graders how to count coins. Prior to beginning the lesson, I took baseline data to understand where my students were. I found that several of my students did not know the names or values of any coins, but there were three who could name the coins and begin to use skip counting to find the value of multiple like coins. I used their knowledge to help guide my lesson, allowing them to practice the correct response and build the lasting understanding I was ultimately striving for.

This stage is also useful when you are out of your comfort zone designing a lesson. Given my own learned helplessness in math, I found it helpful during my practicum placement in high school geometry to root my lesson in the idea of providing students with practical skills that develop understanding about the topic. I knew who my students were from observing and communicating with my mentoring teacher, as well as familiarizing myself with the students' IEP goals, and I knew where my students were going because they would ultimately use geometry in areas of their life outside of high school. In order to root my lesson in the idea of long-term knowledge and practicality, one of my essential questions then was, "Where do we see circumference in everyday life?" and one of my skills was to be able to determine the circumference of everyday objects.

Evaluating Learning

For my ELED 422 lesson plans, creating a performance task along the lines this method suggested worked very well. My colleague and I believed the best way to evaluate the understanding of the students would be for them to take on the role of a museum curator and explain an artifact they would create in their small group that is relevant to and representative of their specific southern colony. Students would choose the colony in their small groups and gather information about it in order to give the presentation to the class. In conjunction with their research and their artifacts, students would go on a museum walk and see artifacts from each of the other groups. To evaluate their performance, they would self-assess their contribution to their small group as well as how the group worked together. Students would also be asked to reflect on connections between the colonies and how their artifact represents their colony's history. They would also be evaluated on a rubric by the teacher and observed during their group work and presentation.

While in my internship, I was finally able to see a lesson plan of this caliber in action. As a review, my fourth-grade students were asked to pick two historical figures from all of the people they had learned about during the year and create puppets of them. The two figures would then have a brief conversation about who they were and what they did. From the beginning, we were meeting students where they were by allowing them to choose their own historical figures. This gave them the opportunity to select characters about which they were confident of their knowledge. Additional supports were available because the students were allowed to work in pairs. In order to present evidence of their learning, their final puppet shows were assessed using a rubric that looked at their historical accuracy as well as the time and effort they put into their puppet. In order to ensure each student had the opportunity and materials to create their puppet, they were given time in class to work. This lesson allowed students to present their own knowledge in a subject they were confident about, as well as watch other students' puppet shows and review with their peers.

I saw another performance task in action in an elementary school resource class while working with fourth-graders on inferences. After walking through a wordless picture book and modeling and then listening to the group's inferences, the students filled out a chart that asked them to write down what they saw in the picture and what inference they made about it. With that chart as a reference sheet, students acted as the author of the book and wrote their own short story about the pictures. It helped that they were writing for students like themselves, because they knew they could be relatively informal. Students were evaluated on a rubric that assessed the relevance of their story—meaning whether or not the student's inferences and story were based on the pictures in the story—if their story had a clear beginning and end, and if their story had correct sequencing.

WHAT WORKED FOR ME: THE W.H.E.R.E.T.O. STRATEGY

Finally, to develop the plan itself for each of the lessons I taught in different settings, I used the Where, Hook, Equip, Revise, self-Evaluate, Tailor, and Organize (W.H.E.R.E.T.O.) (McTighe & Wiggins, 2004) strategy. In the ELED 422 class, this was a guideline available from the sections of the lesson plan template in the *Understanding by Design Professional Development Workbook* (2004).

Where

The objectives of the lesson were the *Where*, as we had to look at *what* students were to accomplish and *how* they would get there. This is similar to the general question I started asking myself with where my students were going and how I could provide the necessary tools to get there. For the colonization plan in ELED 422, those were for the student to understand that the desire for freedom and self-expression can influence where people live, and that students will understand that importance of studying history and its impact on the modern day. For the fourth-grade inferences lesson during practicum, this was for students to understand that making inferences can help them comprehend a situation from just a picture or from little information, and to use those inferences to create a product. For high school geometry, this was understanding the importance of pi in mathematics and how it can help you find things such as circumference. For each of the lessons written in my internship, I focused on how to assist my students in meeting not only their IEP goals but also their own goals.

Hook

The Hook, or activating strategy, is the next step in this model. It is crucial to get students involved quickly, I've found, because without their attention it is difficult to develop understanding. I found that in all subjects, I've gravitated toward asking questions in this area. Having the students think about an answer to something that is novel or hinges on their prior knowledge provides a segue into the lesson. I've learned in my internship that in special education, activating this prior knowledge also helps with the ultimate generalization of the information, because it helps the student think about where they have seen this skill or heard this information used before, and where can they use it in the future.

Equip

In every lesson plan I've written, the Equip portion of the acronym has transferred into the materials needed for the lesson, which is beneficial for relatively scatterbrained people such as me who need to make a list to get anything done. In special education, this is also the portion of the lesson planning where you ask yourself how your students will access the materials. It is crucial to students' learning that they are able to use the materials provided, or that adjustments have been made so they can access the information in a different way with the same result. This relates the materials to knowing your students.

Rethink and Revise

The revising portion of this method is something prospective teachers do not have the opportunity to delve too far into before their internship experience because the ability to teach a longer unit isn't there. Once in my internship, I learned how *difficult* this portion is, but also how *important*. Revising and reflective teaching practices are heavily scrutinized in modern teaching assessments, and for beginning educators like me, it is the most difficult skill to master.

After students have been assessed and progress has been charted, it is important to look over your work and realistically see what worked and what requires improvement. If a student did not understand the material, then it is important to discover what made the knowledge difficult to obtain. Was the pacing too fast for the student? Was something not explained as fully as it should have been? This process can be aided by providing students with the opportunity to ask questions and make suggestions as much as possible.

Self-Evaluation

Rethinking and revising go hand in hand with self-Evaluation, which is a key component to deep understanding. It is important that a student be able to evaluate their own understanding of a topic in order to gauge what they still need to focus on, or what questions they have. In special education, this is particularly important because students are on such varying levels, so tailoring the instruction is crucial.

Tailor

Tailoring is what I have the most experience in, being a special educator. Far beyond their IEPs, though, students still require tailoring of instruction. Students learn in a variety of ways, and as much as possible, information should be presented using a variety of methods in order to make it easier to access for all students. For example, providing a class with *both* a reading *and* a video clip could help students who learn visually and those who learn by poring over a text.

Organize

However, to manage all of this, you have to deal with the step in this sequence that causes me the most trouble: organizing the lesson. In my personal experience, it was difficult for me give all the information in the correct sequence in practice, although I could write it in the planning templates and the lesson plan successfully. This step is important because to help students obtain information, the teacher must have a grasp on what they are teaching. Organizing your lesson in a way that makes sense helps to scaffold instruction and provide students with clear expectations for their learning.

FINAL REFLECTIONS

Without a doubt, the UbD (McTighe & Wiggins, 2004; Wiggins & McTighe, 2005) method of planning a lesson for enduring understanding has helped me focus on what is important in a lesson. When it was introduced in the ELED 422 class, I struggled some with the ideas because it seems idyllic to me. In theory, every student will walk out of the class with a deep understanding of the material regardless of their score on a test, but for some students in my field, that is not something that is possible within one unit or with one overarching performance task. Using the stages presented, I have been able to tailor my instruction to meet the needs of my students, and it has proven more than beneficial, but it does require alteration to meet the needs of all students. Evidence for understanding may not be the same for all students, and the desired results may not be similar for all students. One assessment made me struggle with this idea more than any other: the evaluation of my own teaching.

The edTPA is used to evaluate and assess interns' understanding of their field, knowledge of their students, and how reflective they are as a practitioner. I had seen the three commentaries while in school and understood the principle of the assessment, but it still posed a disheartening task in my internship year. Even though I knew I had all the necessary tools and knowledge to provide my students the means to excel, the question tugged at me: *How do I prove I can teach to someone who has never come into my classroom?* While asking myself that question, it occurred to me that I was ignoring everything I had learned. Through learning the UbD planning method and the W.H.E.R.E.T.O. strategy for writing lesson plans, I had learned that the most important part of my job was to ensure my students were learning—and as long as I knew and could show their progress, then everything else would fall into place. When faced with the edTPA, I briefly forgot that.

In teacher education programs, we are regularly asked to display our understanding of our subject. What the Understanding by Design method asked us to do was plan and reflect on students' knowledge in order to gain holistic information of the students' academic standing. This reflection is what is required by the edTPA. Knowing that I had been equipped with the tools I needed was a great comfort, and keeping in mind that *the most important thing to a teacher is that their students are learning* kept me focused throughout the edTPA process.

On this journey I have learned the essential questions of teaching, and I have learned to question them. I have learned that meeting my students where they are and helping them to where they are going is my most important task as a teacher. Most importantly, I have learned that no assessment can tarnish a passion for educating, and that as long as I focus on teaching, my students, and showing evidence of their learning, my classroom can face any changes to come.

Part II

THE GRADUATE INTERNSHIP YEAR

Kristin T. Rearden

.

Chapter Eight

Getting Started: Orienting and Building Relationships

The pathway for transitioning from student to teacher is often circuitous and always uncharted, as each teacher candidate enters the licensure program with a unique blend of learning experiences, content knowledge, and perspective of what "good teaching" looks like. After years of being primarily on the receiving end of lessons, our teacher candidates must begin to process the spectrum of classroom events from the vantage point of a teacher, ranging from the glaringly obvious reprimand of a student to the subtle communication of academic expectations. This includes awareness of not only what teachers say and do during a lesson but also what they *don't* say or do.

The first section of this chapter describes the approach for setting up the seminar class that supports the field experience. These aspects include the physical design of the seminar classroom, a description of the opening session, and the strategies for preparing the teacher candidates for their classroom experiences. The second section identifies the focal points for observations conducted as part of the field experience, beginning with a description of a possible classroom scenario and then outlining observational protocols. These protocols serve to support teacher candidates' observations and analyses of five aspects of the milieu of teaching: school culture, classroom environment, planning process, instructional strategies, and assessment strategies.

PREPARING FOR THE FIELD EXPERIENCE:
SETTING UP THE SEMINAR CLASS

Physical Design of the Seminar Classroom

Elementary teachers often spend countless hours creating bulletin boards, placing names on items, selecting inspirational and educational placards for the walls, and organizing classroom supplies to prepare for the new school year. The by-product of these concrete endeavors is the establishment of a classroom climate with a foundation for building relationships. College educators, on the other hand, often share a classroom with multiple professors who whisk in and out all day. "Decorating" is not usually an option. Despite this lack of a home base for teaching, I can still communicate important aspects of establishing a positive classroom climate through a few simple steps.

As the teacher candidates arrive on their first day of our preinternship course, they find that the tables are arranged in a U-shape design with a pair of chairs behind each table. Sometimes that means scrambling to make the table and chair arrangements during the fifteen minutes between class sessions held in that room! In front of each chair, there is a name tag for each student so they know exactly where to sit. By setting up the room this way, I am conveying two messages within the first sixty seconds of class. The first message is that I was anticipating their arrival by having a place ready for each of them. Just as many elementary classrooms have desks, cubbies, and hooks already identified with students' names, I've prepared a place for each teacher candidate. Think about arriving at a formal wedding reception, or a Thanksgiving meal with an extended family, or perhaps a dinner party with good friends. In many of these kinds of social situations, you have a table number or place card with your name on it, indicating where you will be sitting during the meal. Someone was expecting you, and acknowledged ahead of time that you were partaking in the event. In the same way, even at the college level, I am trying to convey that message before I even verbalize a greeting beyond just "Good morning!" Through the name tags, I am saying: "Welcome to our course; I was expecting you. I am glad you're here." Wong and Wong advocate for assigning seats in their widely circulated publication *The First Days of School* (1998) for similar reasons.

The second message I am conveying is through the arrangement of the tables. The chairs are not all facing forward; they are not clustered around tables in groups of four around the room. Instead, they are arranged behind tables in a U-shape so that each student can easily see every other student. Backs do not have to be twisted to see someone else talk. The teacher is not the only person who is easily visible. The message communicated is: We are here to learn from each other. So within the first sixty seconds, I have hopefully sent two nonverbal messages to the candidates: You were expected, and your input is valued.

The Opening Class Session

From the class roll, I know only the names of the teacher candidates in the course. I may have met them in advising sessions prior to the semester, but even with that background, I do not know them, nor do they know me. To begin the introductions, I ask the teacher candidates to share three pieces of information about themselves: their name; something unique about themselves, such as a hobby; and the name of their kindergarten, first-grade, or second-grade teacher. As we go around the room, teacher candidates state their names, they share their unique features, and then, as per the directions, they identify one of their earliest teachers. A few candidates who moved frequently have trouble recalling an early teacher, especially if they were in more than one school during their primary grades, but most can recall (often fondly) the names of their primary grade teachers.

After we've gone around the room, I then ask, "Who can remember the name of the governor of your state during your early elementary years?" No hands. The head of a major corporation? Still no hands. OK, the mayor of their town or city? Still no hands. My point in asking these questions is that there is a small sphere of people who have direct influence on the life of a young child. A teacher is one of those people. Though a teacher will not command the six-figure salary of a corporate CEO, and will rarely have the opportunity for much public recognition, it is this person—not the CEO or politician—who will be remembered long after those whom society deems as powerful. Teachers are forever in the memories of their students. Though not typically reflected by wealth or public recognition, the impact of a teacher is powerful. The influence of a single teacher cannot be taken lightly! I hope to help them recognize their potential impact early in their teaching career.

Preparing to Enter the Schools: First Impressions

Prior to starting the field experience, our seminar discussions focus on several aspects of professionalism. Not surprisingly, the initial aspect is the importance of first impressions. This begins with "virtual" first impressions, as they will send an introductory email to their mentoring teacher. Expressing gratitude for a mentor's willingness to allow others into his or her classroom is a must! I want our candidates to always to be mindful of the guest status they have in another teacher's classroom, and hope that some day they will return the favor to other teacher candidates. Similarly, I model this expression of gratitude through an email to each of their mentors, copied to the teacher candidates and principals. In this email, I also clearly communicate the expectations of our teacher candidates and mentors, schedules, and contact information. The importance of explicit communication about logistics, and our expressions of gratitude to these mentoring teachers who are willing to "pay it forward" to support the next generation of teachers, cannot be overemphasized.

The next aspect is in-person first impressions—what to wear and what not to wear. Part of this conversation depends on the culture of the schools, but there are certain conventions that supersede location. Simply stated, we want the teacher candidates' attire to project "I am a professional" rather than "I just got off the treadmill" or "I am ready for the beach." In some cases, staff members wear the same uniform-style items that their students wear, such as school polo shirts and khaki pants. While the teacher candidates don't purchase those items, they can certainly wear similarly colored shirts and pants to establish themselves as part of the school community.

We also address cell phone etiquette. Some of these candidates have had phones for a decade—or more—and it is challenging for them to break from accessing social media, emailing, or texting for even four hours. Teacher candidates can be encouraged to bring a folder for school papers and a notebook for recording observations. Using a notebook instead of a smartphone or tablet device can reduce the potential for interacting with electronics instead of the world around them.

Examples of items on our "Do" list for the school-based visits include:

- Make an initial contact with your mentor by email prior to your first visit.
- Arrive on time (or a little early) for each classroom visit.
- Learn names of students and staff.
- Dress professionally.
- Avoid using your cell phone for the duration of the visit.

Examples on our "Don't" list include:

- Criticize your mentor's classroom management or instructional strategies directly to him/her, or speak disparagingly of previous mentors or teachers.
- Refuse opportunities to interact with students in small groups or short, prepared lessons.
- Be disruptive in the classroom (engaging in conversations with students while they should be working; answering a ringing cell phone).

THE FIELD EXPERIENCE

During their preinternship semester, our elementary teacher candidates spend four hours each week in local elementary schools. They are assigned to a primary-level classroom at one school for six weeks, and an intermediate-level classroom at a different school for six weeks. When classrooms are assigned, the candidates are placed in pairs. This allows candidates to "debrief" on a weekly basis with someone who has been exposed to the same setting. This model has been implemented in student teaching (Kamens, 2007) and supports our focus of developing reflective practitioners. Comparing observation notes and inferences made from those observations allows the teacher candidates to view situations from not only their perspective but also an alternative vantage point. Logistically, this strategy also reduces the number of requests we need to make for mentor teachers.

The Spectrum of Classroom Environments

Each classroom is a unique environment. From the descriptions below, consider two possibilities for a fifth-grade classroom in which a teacher candidate could be placed for conducting an observation.

The teacher stands by the classroom door and greets students as they enter from the adjacent fifth-grade classroom. The students stop by their classroom mailboxes to see if there are any papers to put in their folders. Then they go to their seats, take out their math textbooks and notebooks, and copy the lesson objective that is displayed on the white board. Their textbooks are open to the page listed under the lesson objective. There is a familiar song playing, and they know that when the song ends, they should have those tasks completed and be ready for the lesson. During this time, the teacher has not uttered a single direction. The song ends, and the teacher begins the lesson by asking the designated student leader of the day to read the lesson objective to the class.

In the adjacent fifth-grade classroom, students enter boisterously and haphazardly. They meander through the room, talking and congregating in clusters. The teacher strives to get their attention and have them sit at their desks. Slowly, students shuffle to their desks as conversations linger. Eventually all are seated, though most are still talking. Again, the teacher asks for attention. Students quiet down, and she asks them to open their notebooks to the next blank page and open their textbooks to a certain page number. She repeats the page number three times before all students have their books open to that day's lesson. She begins to write the lesson objective on the board and asks students to copy it in their notebooks. Several students ask others nearby if they can borrow pencils, and several more go to the pencil sharpener. The teacher stands in the front of the classroom and waits for all students to copy down the lesson objective. Seven minutes have elapsed, and some students are still copying the lesson objective.

From a brief observation period in either of these classrooms, a teacher candidate could analyze classroom procedures, communication strategies, and time on task. Ideally, we want our teacher candidates to be placed with mentors who have classrooms that reflect the first scenario rather than the "how I don't want my classroom to run" approach to classroom observations. Fortunately, we have a very strong rapport with our school-based partners and are able to place our teacher candidates in classrooms where they can analyze what is working and why, rather than what is not effective and why not. Additionally, by varying both the grade level and the school location during their field experience, teacher candidates can see similarities and differences in teaching styles firsthand. Demographics, school communities, classroom resources, and teaching styles can be compared and contrasted.

To support candidates with observing and analyzing the milieu of teaching, they complete several protocols that require obtaining data, making observations, conducting interviews, and reflecting on the information. The protocols are adapted from the field experience handbook for our elementary licensure program (University of Tennessee Office of Field-Based Experiences, 2013). They encompass the following five focal points, each of which will each be addressed in detail: school culture, classroom environment, the planning process, instructional strategies, and assessment strategies.

Focal Point One: School Culture

As part of their field experience, teacher candidates observe and investigate several sociocultural aspects of each school setting. Figure 8.1 includes some of the prompts for this observation. The mix of factual, observational, and reflective prompts allows candidates to discern information in various ways. School websites can provide information regarding student population, building construction, and staff numbers. Observations of interactions between and among mentoring teachers, other grade-level teachers, teacher assistants, resource teachers, and administrators provide a glimpse into the nature and purpose of those gatherings and conversations. The reflective component pertains to comparisons between the candidate's own experience in primary or intermediate grades and the field experience classrooms. This provides the candidates with an opportunity to note both differences and similarities.

One area that surprises most teacher candidates is how two schools in the same district can be so different. Their first field experience in a classroom might be a relatively new building in which teachers have their own office adjacent to the classroom, students have their own cubbies for storage, classrooms are fully equipped with multiple technology resources, and the library has space for computers, print material, and whole-group instruction. Their second placement school might be a seventy-year-old structure with a teacher's desk in the corner of the classroom, storage in the hallway for coats and books, cart-based technology resources shared among all staff, and a library

Socio-Cultural Context of the Elementary School

Consider the following questions as you observe each learning community. Write your response directly under each question.

<u>**School Observations**</u>

1. What is the name of the elementary school where are you observing? Where is it located?

2. Identify the socio-economic status of the community.

3. How many students and faculty are at this school? How many teachers at each grade level?

4. Describe the physical characteristics of the school (when built, layout, etc.).

5. Describe the support staff and specific programs offered to students, such as English language support.

6. How are grouping and tracking done at your grade level? How are children placed in these groups? Can they move from one ability group to another? How? Who makes these decisions?

7. What interactions have you observed between teachers and administrators?

8. How does this school compare to the school you attended?

Figure 8.1. Prompts for Observation of Sociocultural Aspects of School Setting

with limited storage and seating. One school may have nearly all students receiving free breakfast and lunch, while 90 percent of the students in the other school either purchase or bring their lunches. These schools may be in the same district and only a few miles apart, but their cultures are distinctly different. The appreciation of each school's unique culture is an important aspect to viewing the contextual components of the teaching profession.

Focal Point Two: The Classroom Environment

During the field experience, teacher candidates conduct two observations of the classroom environment. For the first observation, they focus on aspects such as the physical setup of the classroom and the classroom procedures. Figure 8.2 lists the field note prompts for the first classroom environment observation.

Once the teacher candidates have observed these aspects of the classroom, they observe the second component of the classroom environment: classroom

---

Classroom Environment I

Classroom Design: Sketch a map of the classroom indicating desk arrangement, computers, classroom supplies, centers, etc.

Opening Routines
A. Attendance, lunch count, folder collection
B. Calendar, morning message, daily schedule posting, other

Operating Procedures
A. Walking to/from specials
B. Leaving during class time
C. Sharpening pencils, getting supplies
D. Emergency Drills

Teaching Routines
A. Expected classroom behavior (what aspects are consistent? what aspects depend on the activity?)
B. Noise level expectations
C. Discussion procedures (raise hands, chant responses, call out, mix)
D. Passing out papers/materials distribution (student job, teacher job, or mix)
E. Marking and grading assignments (immediate feedback, collection of work, mix)

Closing Routines
A. Putting away supplies, equipment
B. Collecting work
C. Transitioning to next lesson

General Comments on Classroom Routines

Figure 8.2. Prompts for Observation of Physical Environment of Classroom

management. This is when many of the teacher candidates experience the head-on collision between theory and practice. In theory, well-organized classrooms should run smoothly and seamlessly, with students graciously complying with the teacher's first request of any directive and remaining on task throughout the lesson. In reality, most classrooms reflect a different picture. Teacher candidates focus their observations on both the overt and the subtle means by which mentors strive to maximize students' time on task, whether students are working in a whole-group setting, small-group setting, or individually. Aspects to document for the second classroom environment observation include instructional strategies and routines for maximizing students' time on task.

As they are making these observations, teacher candidates are also noting specific behavior management strategies. They may observe a mentor teacher directly or indirectly addressing behavior throughout a lesson. Noting a mentor teacher's system for consequences and rewards is also important for teacher candidates. Management systems consist of recognizing positive behavior and stemming behavior that is off task or disruptive, and again, teacher candidates need to see the interplay between theory and practice. In discussing management systems with their mentor teachers, they often discover that these strategies are reconfigured over time as behaviors change, incentives decrease in effectiveness, or consequences no longer make an impact. Figure 8.3 lists sample prompts for the second classroom environment observation.

Focal Point Three: The Planning Process

In the general methods course, Colleen focuses on the "backwards design" (Wiggins & McTighe, 2005) format for planning (see chapters 2 to 5). During one of the field placement sessions, teacher candidates have the option of either interviewing their mentor teacher or observing a lesson for evidence of planning elements. We want the teacher candidates to hear the *why* of the planning process just as much as we want them to hear the *what*. Why was this assessment selected over others? Why was this format selected for the structure of the lesson? What factors influenced the group composition? How did the mentor teacher know to teach Y before X, even though it's presented in the curriculum guide as X before Y? All of these probes into a mentor teacher's planning process are so important for a new teacher.

Planning decisions are often derived from a blend of professional development opportunities, professional literature, peer mentoring, and trial and error. The information that teacher candidates can obtain about planning through this "window" will become even more important during their internship when they are the ones teaching the lessons; for now, we just want our

---

Classroom Environment II

Instructional Activity Routine
A. Activities to do when work is completed
B. Student time-on-task
C. Out-of-seat policies
D. Expectations for answering questions or adding to discussions

Group Activity Routine
A. Expected behavior in groups
B. Individual responsibilities
C. Student-student interactions

Academic Feedback Routine
A. Rewards and incentives
B. Posting student work
C. Communicating with parents
D. Written comments on assignments

Management Strategies
A. Non-verbal control
B. Overlooking of inconsequential actions
C. Administering consequences for infractions
D. Awareness of potential problems: use of proximity, verbal cues, directly addressing

Posted Classroom Rules:

List of Consequences for Misbehavior:

Figure 8.3.   Prompts for Observation of Behavioral Environment of Classroom

teacher candidates to realize that planning for lessons entails so much more than opening a teacher's edition of a textbook.

To guide the mentor teacher interview, the teacher candidates are provided with prompts pertaining to three aspects of planning: the lesson objective, the instructional activities, and the assessments. They can expand the interview protocol beyond the sample questions. In some cases, the teacher candidates are unable to conduct a full interview, so the planning protocol also contains a set of supplementary observation questions for teacher candidates to note during a lesson. Based on these observations, they could follow up with more targeted questions for their mentors. The planning observation still focuses on the same three areas as the interview: the lesson objectives, instructional activities, and assessments. Figure 8.4 includes suggested interview prompts and observation questions.

After observing the lesson, the teacher candidate can follow up with the mentor teacher to ask specific questions, such as, "Even though the lesson objective seemed very challenging to the students at first, most seemed to demonstrate mastery at the end of the lesson. How did you know it was an

---

The Planning Process

Interview Questions

- **Lesson objective.** What is the lesson objective? How did you know it was appropriate for the students?

- **Instructional activities.** How will all students be engaged in the lesson? Will all students attempt the same task? Will other subject areas be incorporated? How will technology be utilized?

- **Assessments.** How will you measure mastery? Does mastery look the same for every student? Are there multiple measures with different formats? Do students have a choice about demonstrating their understanding?

Observation Focal Points

- **Lesson objectives.** How is the lesson objective communicated to students? Do students record the objective? Is there any discussion about why the objective is important to students?

- **Instructional activities.** Is there evidence of differentiation? Were students given opportunities for successful completion of learning tasks? Were other disciplines incorporated?

- **Assessments.** What evidence demonstrates the effectiveness of the lesson? Were students given enough opportunities to demonstrate what they had learned?

Figure 8.4.   Prompts for Exploring the Planning Process

appropriate objective?" This could lead to a brief discussion about the use of pretest data, previous experience with troubleshooting potential issues pro-actively, or the use of research-based strategies for teaching that particular concept—in other words, some of the *why* behind the planning process that is so vital to developing effective lessons. After seeing the behind-the-scenes effort to create lessons, it does not take long for the teacher candidates to recognize the daunting task of planning. When considering the challenges of teaching, Mackenzie wrote:

> The greatest challenge that I think I'll face as a teacher is planning, especially my first few years in the classroom. I'm very dedicated to everything that I do and fear that I'll let planning lessons take over my life.

Focal Point Four: Instructional Strategies

During one observed lesson, teacher candidates focus solely on the mentor teacher's actions during a lesson. The realm of a classroom is so complex, particularly at the elementary level, so they are provided with a list of items to guide the observation process. Figure 8.5 contains a list of items to observe. Our main goal for this observation is to recognize the impact of various facets of instruction, such as communication strategies, movement throughout the room, and lesson flow. By scripting a lesson from start to end and completing an observation checklist, teacher candidates can not only note what happens in a classroom but also start to analyze why certain events occur. For ex-ample, a teacher candidate may record the observation of her mentor teacher closely monitoring students during group work by constantly circulating throughout the room and asking probing questions as she circulates. Based on these notes, the teacher candidate can infer that the monitoring might serve two purposes: ensuring students are on task, and checking for understanding of the task on which they are working.

During our seminar, this single observation and set of inferences can lead us to an important discussion about a teacher's role during a student-centered instructional component. How would that classroom look if the teacher sat at her desk to grade papers while students worked on their group projects? What can the mentor teacher learn by monitoring that would not be known just from viewing the final product? How else can individual accountability during group work be monitored? Discussing the benefits of a teacher's ac-tive engagement in the context of a lesson observation provides context for the teacher candidates. Rather than an abstract idea of what it means to be an engaged teacher, we can now focus on what was observed in a classroom setting with real students and real outcomes. They can watch firsthand what

---

Instructional Strategies

1. Use of set (such as opening question, statement of the objectives)

2. Use of closure (such as summary, restating the objective)

3. Check for understanding

4. Monitoring learning tasks

5. Amount of teacher talk (extensive, moderate, minimal)

6. Amount of student talk/response patterns (individuals volunteering, group responses, random selection)

7. Games (review, guided practice)

8. Group and cooperative learning activities

9. Use of audio-visuals and technology

10. Use of transitions

11. Support for varied ability levels

General comments on instructional strategies:

Figure 8.5. Prompts for Exploring Instructional Strategies

occurs when mentor teachers "work" the classroom and monitor students who are engaging with the material.

In her written reflection, Kathleen noted how the management skills of her mentor teacher impacted instruction:

My mentor in my second placement uses centers frequently, having a math and literacy rotation in the morning and a science and social studies rotation in the

afternoon. In between the center work, she has whole-class instruction and activities. While the students were at their centers, she was able to take one group
at a time and work on specific skills. It was clear to me from the beginning that
her classroom management skills make this type of structure possible—the students know what is expected of them and respect one another. When asking my
mentor how she is able to do this, she replied, "Model, model, model, model,
model."

Focal Point Five: Assessment Strategies

Similar to the planning focus, teacher candidates have the option of either
interviewing the mentor teacher or observing the assessment components
of a lesson. For the interview, probes focus on assessment at the classroom,
district, and state levels. If an interview is not possible, teacher candidates observe a lesson for assessment elements. When observing a lesson, the teacher
candidates should be able to identify the concept or process that the students
should know at the end of a lesson or sequence of lessons, and describe how
the students will demonstrate their mastery of that concept or process. Figure
8.6 contains suggested questions for the interview protocol and the observation focal points for assessment.

Regarding assessment, the teacher candidates are keenly aware of the pressure facing their mentor teachers—and all teachers—with the trend of tying
teacher pay to student performance on standardized tests. They have heard
about this in their classes and most likely through the media. During the
field experience, they may see how this pressure is manifested in elementary
school schedules that do not allocate designated time for science and social
studies instruction in order to focus more time on math and literacy instruction. They may also see it in the kinds of instruction implemented, such as
lessons that focus more on test preparation than deep understanding. Kathleen
noted this in both her intermediate-level placement and her primary placement, and considered the implications:

> At the intermediate level, a challenge that many teachers face of course is the
> introduction of standardized state tests. At the primary level, in first grade . . .
> there are other standardized tests that are taken throughout the year. Throughout
> both experiences, the two most frequently discussed issues were those of evalu-
> ations and standardized testing. . . . The biggest challenge that I believe comes
> out of this is how to juggle making sure that your students understand the con-
> tent thoroughly and are engaged with making sure that they are well equipped
> to perform well on the test. I think it easy to fall into the trap of "teaching to the
> test" instead of focusing on in-depth, meaningful learning that will promote life-
> long learning. However, one of the great things about teachers is their ability to
> problem solve. If there is anyone who can find the right balance—teachers can.

Assessment Strategies

Interview Questions:

State and district level: What tests are administered, and how are the data used?

Classroom level: How are diagnostic tests used for planning? How are summative tests used for planning? What kinds of formal and informal assessments do you use?

Observation Focal Points:

Pre-assessments: Is there evidence that diagnostic data were used in creating the lesson?

Informal assessments: How does the mentor teacher check for understanding during a lesson? Are there examples of both individual and group responses when checking for understanding through questioning?

Formal assessments: What formats were used? Were multiple opportunities given for students to demonstrate mastery? Were the expectations for mastery communicated? Did the assessments match the lesson objective?

Individual accountability: If students were working in groups, were individual students held accountable? If so, how?

Higher-order thinking: Were there examples of opportunities for promoting higher-order thinking in the assessments?

Figure 8.6.   Prompts for Exploring Assessment Strategies

FINAL REFLECTIONS

During the spring block semester prior to their internship, the teacher candidates spend approximately forty-eight hours in a classroom, with twenty-four hours each at their two placement schools. Throughout the field experience, they have observed, recorded, and reflected. They have witnessed congruence and dissonance between theory and practice. They have compared and contrasted their placements as well as connected experiences with their own personal backgrounds in school. These initial classroom immersions provide the foundation they need to begin considering the grade-level band, school environment, and teaching style that they envision for themselves.

One outcome for many of the teacher candidates was that they were able to discern the grade-level band for which they seemed best suited. After considering her observations in both a primary- and intermediate-level classroom, Alana determined where she felt she'd fit best:

> Being in both classrooms and seeing what I liked specifically about each one helped me realize that I would like to teach middle elementary grades.

For Mackenzie, the field experience provided her with a realistic view of the profession she was about to enter:

> When reflecting on this semester's practicum, I've realized that the time spent in the classroom was extremely eye-opening and informative. Prior to this class, I had many preconceived notions about the role of the teacher and the challenges I would be facing. Having the opportunity to get to know two elementary school teachers and spend time in the classroom was a great way to clear up my assumptions and learn about what it's really like being a teacher. . . . This practicum was a great opportunity to see what being a teacher is really about rather than just reading about it in textbooks.

Many candidates' final reflections noted how they felt prepared to begin their internship. Chloe noted how both the coursework and field experience prepared her for the upcoming year:

> My practicum experience, in addition to a full course load of education classes, has allowed me to observe real teaching and real students that exemplify what I have been learning all semester. This opportunity to observe two elementary schools in [this school system] has opened my eyes to the many aspects of the public school system in general. The combination of my active participation in practicum and knowledge I have learned in my classes have served as preparation for my internship year.

Although the teacher candidates can't fully envision all that the internship will entail, they exit the preinternship semester with a more realistic view of the demands—and joys—of teaching.

Chapter Nine

Fall Semester: Overlaying Effective Teaching with TEAM Rubrics

Once the school year has commenced, our teacher candidates are referred to as *interns*. They hold state-issued interim teaching licenses, complete background checks and drug screenings, and start on the first day of in-service just like their mentors. The yearlong internship provides nearly ten months to observe, coteach, and teach under the guidance of a mentor and university supervisor. In this chapter, we'll focus on the first semester of the internship.

In the first section of this chapter, we'll describe the initial weeks of the internship. In what ways does the physical space of a classroom matter? How do interns establish their teaching credibility right from the start? How do interns gradually assume responsibility for planning and teaching? In the second section, we'll focus on the strategies we use to support interns' planning skills. In what ways do an intern's plans differ from a mentor's plans? What questions should interns ask themselves and their mentors as they plan? In the final two sections, we'll look at how we prepare the interns for their first formal teaching evaluations by starting with effective teaching strategies *first* and overlaying the rubrics (such as edTPA) by which they are evaluated *second*. This is at the heart of our approach to preparing teachers: effective teaching is effective teaching, regardless of the rubrics or checklists by which they are evaluated.

INITIAL WEEKS OF THE INTERNSHIP

Physical Space Considerations

If you have shared a small dorm room or apartment with someone who has a very different perspective on cleanliness or organization, you can appreciate how important it is for interns and mentors to have similar approaches to the physical setup of a classroom. Our mentors are required to be excellent role models for teaching with a certain amount of experience, both of which are quantifiable attributes. However, we also consider qualitative attributes when matching interns with mentors. One main consideration is compatible organizational strategies. When matching interns and mentors, we strive to pair organizationally like-minded people together. Interns who color-coded their planners and are never without their accordion file of purposefully placed papers will not fare well in classrooms that, from the outside looking in, appear to be highly disorganized. Stacks of papers, projects, manipulatives, and supplies across all available horizontal surfaces would bother some interns but not others.

For sixteen or more years, the interns have been on the receiving end of first-day-of-school experiences. They have entered classrooms that were decorated, organized, and personalized. As described in chapter 8, even our field experience seminar classroom had name tags and assigned seats for each of them; they obtained a syllabus, pertinent handouts, and names of their field placement schools and mentors in the first week. Even so, interns are often surprised at the amount of work it takes to prepare a classroom. After the first two weeks of school, Amelia noted her realization about this:

> I knew there would be things I needed to do other than planning for lessons, but I didn't realize how many other important things there are to do! I knew the first few days were mostly for time to set up our classrooms, but I had no idea how many things had to be done each year to set it up. I also never realized how much thought went into individualizing things for each student, such as name tags, cubby labels, folders, composition books, etc. . . . I suppose I should have known that all of these were things that the teachers had to do and they did not just magically appear, but I had just not really thought much about it. It is a lot to do, but it was definitely worth it once I saw the students come in and feel some ownership after seeing their names throughout the classroom.

They knew that these items did not "magically appear," as Amelia described. Interestingly, however, most of the interns did not consider the time and effort put forth by their teachers at the start of each school year until they were the ones getting a classroom ready for students. They also developed an appreciation for the match between their mentor's organizational style and theirs if they have a rotational mentor (with whom they work for a six-week period for broadening their grade-level experiences) whose idea of organization differs from theirs. As described by Amelia:

> Not only is (organization) helpful for the teacher, but it is good for the students too. I think it is important for both the teacher and the students to know where

everything is and not have to spend a lot of time searching for things. My mentor in first grade is extremely organized and I think that helps to make every day run smoother. My (rotational) mentor was not very organized. Both [the mentor] and the students often did not know where things were and spent a lot of time searching for things around the classroom. This took a lot of time away from instruction and the students often became distracted with other things and it was sometimes difficult to get them back on task.

Finally, it's helpful for the intern to have his or her own "space," whether that space is a small desk in the corner of the classroom or a portion of a counter in a classroom office. Just as students have their desks, hooks, and cubbies to establish their place in the classroom, interns also need an area set aside for their personal and professional belongings. Mentors and interns should discuss the organizational setup of a classroom prior to the first day for students. The location of the intern's work area, the storage area for extra school supplies, the system for collecting and storing student work, and the arrangement of student desks can all be discussed so that the intern is clear about the mentor's preferences for organization.

Establishing a Presence

By the time we have our first graduate class session on campus in August, the interns have spent approximately two weeks in their placement classroom already, as they follow the local school district's calendar for their internship. However, by this point, I have already met with their principals and mentors to establish our partnership and collaborate on a shared vision for the interns' professional development. One important component of acclimating interns is to ensure that both students and parents view them as teachers. Suggestions include:

- Posting both the mentor teacher's name and the intern's name on the class-room door.
- Introducing the intern as a second teacher in the classroom.
- Having the intern take an active role, such as greeting the students, giving directions for a task or classroom procedure, and taking the lunch count during the first week to ensure personal interactions early on.
- Including both names on back-to-school informational handouts and on class websites, along with brief biographical sketches to highlight the intern's educational background.

In addition to providing opportunities for interactions, these steps can support the interns with establishing credibility among students and parents.

Top Ten Ways to Help Your Interns Succeed This Year

10. Recognize the dichotomy between their university world and their internship world. It does exist, and they will struggle with the demands of each.

9. Remind them that you may not need lesson plans, but they do. Learning to plan a lesson is like learning how to drive. They are novices still figuring out which is the brake pedal and which is the gas pedal; you are veterans who are eating, talking on your cell phone, and changing the radio station while merging on highways. Articulate your thoughts about planning as much as possible!

8. Prior to initial lessons, talk about strategies and review their lesson plan together. Be sure the lesson plan is based on standards (state, county, etc). Ask questions when you see red flags ("Kindergarten students will sit and listen attentively to the lecture for the duration of the 45-min lesson.")

7. Notify them well in advance about rotating school-based duties such as bus duty or lunch duty, or after-school events such as team planning sessions. Present it as a duty ("We have bus duty next week"), not as an invitation ("Would you like to lose even more sleep and join me early in the morning to stand around and watch kids disembark from buses?").

6. Expect them to arrive on time every day and leave at the appropriate time every day, to call in sick as needed, and to give advance notice for the two allotted personal days (not counting interview days in late spring). There should be no deviation from this except for occasional medical appointments or family needs. If you stay after school for planning purposes, interns

---

Figure 9.1a.   Suggestions for Mentors to Support Intern Success

Since many of the interns will be recent college graduates, their young age can make them appear naïve and uninformed about education. However, given their backgrounds in undergraduate coursework, their field experiences, and their prior paid or volunteer work with children, they are far from unprepared for the role they are entering. Their mentors clearly have more experience and pedagogical background, and it's important for mentors to communicate that they—not the interns—are identified as the teachers of record for students' legal documentation. Nevertheless, establishing the cred-

should also stay one day a week for that purpose. They are also responsible for quite a bit of UT coursework and some hold evening jobs to be able to spend the entire year in an unpaid internship, so please discuss after-school expectations with them so both of you are on the same page about it.

5. Include them in parent meetings to see how you handle irate, upset, happy, confused, and/or frustrated caregivers. They should not initiate any meeting, but should be present.

4. Listen and respond to their concerns with rephrasing, acknowledgement, encouragement and questioning in addition to responding with advice. Sometimes interns just need to verbalize their feelings and frustrations and are not looking for answers.

3. Co-teach, turn teach, co-plan, turn plan, co-assess and turn assess before they lead. If they are leading, see #9 and #8.

2. Give them feedback on lessons after the students are out of earshot or out of the room. The feedback should accentuate the positive and clearly state the negative. Including both promotes growth. Focusing on only one creates divas or despair.

1. Help them stay positive and flexible through modeling. You are a huge influence on their perspective of what it takes to be a great teacher!

Figure 9.1b.   Suggestions for Mentors to Support Intern Success

ibility of the intern early in the year can help students view both the mentor and intern as equally deserving of respect.

I also provide mentors with a list of ideas for supporting their interns throughout the year (see figure 9.1). This list of ten items is particularly helpful for new mentors. It approaches the topic of intern support in a condensed fashion as compared to the university handbook that we provide to every mentor. The interns receive a parallel version of this to communicate the same information from their perspective (see figure 9.2).

Top Ten Ways to Survive the Internship Year

10. Acknowledge that you now live in three worlds: the university world, the internship world, and your personal world. Each will vie for your time and attention, so prioritize on a daily basis.

9. Be organized. Buy/use a planner to keep track of the various important dates in your three worlds. Write down everything.

8. Be prepared. Your mentor may not need lesson plans, but you do. Learning to plan a lesson is like learning how to drive. Interns are novices still figuring out which is the brake pedal and which is the gas pedal; mentors are veterans who are eating, talking on their cell phones, and changing the radio station while merging on highways. Ask questions about planning often if your mentor is not "planning out loud."

7. Be your own advocate. If you don't think you have enough teaching responsibilities, think you are spending too much time in the copier room, or are unsure of expectations, communicate your concerns to someone who can resolve the issue.

6. Take care of yourself. Take vitamins and/or eat healthily as much as possible, wash your hands often, don't short-change your sleep, find time to pursue exercise or your favorite hobby, find someone with an encouraging attitude to whom you can briefly vent, and recognize when you are getting worn down.

5. Be professional. Arrive on time every day and leave at the appropriate time every day, call in sick as needed, and give advance notice for the two allotted personal days (not counting interview days in late spring). There should be no deviation from this except for occasional medical appointments or family

---

Figure 9.2a. Suggestions for Intern Success

Assuming Responsibility for Planning, Teaching, and Assessing

Although the mentor is the teacher of record, both the mentor and intern share the responsibility of educating the students. This does not look the same at the beginning, middle, and end of the school year. Over time, there should be a gradual assumption of planning, teaching, and assessment responsibilities. Even in a semester-long student teaching experience, there should be a proportional relationship between the amount of time in a classroom and the

needs. If your mentor stays after school for planning purposes, you should also stay one day a week for that purpose. Discuss after-school expectations with your mentor so both of you are on the same page about it. Be a team player with both instructional and non-instructional duties.

4. Be ready for ups and downs. You will feel overwhelmed, elated, triumphant, and defeated – possibly all in the same day, but definitely at various points in the year. Feeling overwhelmed is different from feeling miserable. If you are truly unhappy about your placement or your career choice, communicate those sentiments to discern whether it's a fleeting sentiment or grounded in questions about your future plans.

3. Listen actively and communicate professionally. Resolve issues in person - not via email, text messages, or Facebook.

2. Be reflective. You will receive feedback on lessons by many different people, starting with your own reflections! Critical feedback should never be construed as, or given as, a personal affront but rather as a step towards growing professionally.

1. Keep your students at the forefront. It is easy to slide into negativity when you are unpaid, overwhelmed with course work, struggling financially and feeling underappreciated. However, the year will be challenging and extremely rewarding if you choose to embrace every opportunity for becoming a great teacher. Surround yourself with positive people and keep sight of the reason you entered the profession: your students!

Figure 9.2b.   Suggestions for Intern Success

teaching opportunities—the longer the interns are in the classroom, the more responsibility they should have.

Similar to the field experience observational protocols, the observations during the initial days in the classroom focus on the mentor's strategies and procedures. How are classroom rules established and maintained? Where do students turn in homework? What information is posted on the whiteboard each day? What are the morning routines for students as they enter the classroom? Although the interns and mentors have probably discussed what these aspects will look like, it's important for interns to observe the actual implementation before taking responsibility for these procedural components.

Once the intern has observed these aspects, they must be able to put them into practice. Maintaining the same routines and communicating the same expectations as their mentors is imperative, as noted by Samantha:

> The one tip that I have learned about classroom management that I would like to share with other interns is set your behavior expectations prior to a lesson or activity. At the beginning of the internship, I did not do this and I paid the price.

No mentor or supervisor wants interns to "pay the price," as Samantha stated, since that "price" is lost instructional time and a diminished presence in the classroom. Rather, we want to see the interns seamlessly transition into the role of the lead teacher for longer periods of time and more complex lessons. Although observations support teacher development, they will learn more about teaching—and themselves—while teaching than while studying or observing (Merseth, Sommer, & Dickstein, 2008).

To facilitate this transition, we provide the interns and mentors with a suggested calendar for transitioning from observations to coteaching to lead teaching. The calendar is presented as a discussion tool rather than a requirement for strict adherence, recognizing that each classroom and teaching pair is unique. Table 9.1 provides a suggested calendar for the first four weeks of the school year.

DEVELOPING PLANNING SKILLS

Pat Summitt, the highly successful women's basketball coach for the University of Tennessee Lady Vols, is known for the adage: "Offense sells tickets. Defense wins games" (Miller & Coffey, 2009, p. 117). My education-based version of this coaching strategy is: "Activities generate excitement. Planning fosters learning." In other words, it's not sufficient to just find a creative teaching idea on the Internet and insert it into a lesson plan. Effective teaching—that is, teaching that supports the desired student outcomes—requires extensive planning, from the first to the final seconds of the lesson.

Lesson Plans: Novice and Veteran Approaches

For a new teacher, the process of planning lessons requires a significant amount of time. Mentors, on the other hand, may have no written plans other than the lesson objective and page number of a textbook. With the benefit

Table 9.1.   Suggested Calendar for Beginning of Internship

Week	Intern/Mentor Actions
1 *(in-service week in fall)*	*Intern*: Meet the school staff; participate in all in-service events; assist with preparing the classroom. *Mentor*: Familiarize your intern with the school culture through staff introductions and building tours; be sure your intern is included on schedules and knows the routines for nonteaching responsibilities of staff, such as bus duty, recess duty, car line, etc.
2 *(first week with students)*	*Intern*: Become familiar with students and routines through active participation as well as observations; learn students' names; lead short, recurrent events such as calendar time or morning message; ask your mentor to "think out loud" as he or she plans for the week; observe how your mentor establishes routines such as how students should obtain supplies or exit the classroom. *Mentor*: Introduce your intern as another teacher in the classroom; include your intern's name with yours on all communication, such as introductory notes to parents and on the class website; "think out loud" during planning time.
3	*Intern*: Continue with leading short, recurrent events; discuss organizational routines or procedures about which you have any questions; coplan for one content area by collaborating with your mentor. *Mentor*: Share the "why" behind decisions made through analysis of diagnostic testing as you make placements for leveled groups; "think out loud" with your intern as you plan for one subject, articulating decisions about learner outcomes, pacing, materials, and assessments.
4	*Intern*: Continue with recurrent events; coteach the subject area that you coplanned; coplan for a new subject area; reflect on teaching. *Mentor*: Provide feedback about the coteaching experience; coplan for a new subject area; share strategies for long-term planning.

of years of experience, mentors can execute a lesson seamlessly—knowing what questions to ask, where students are most likely to struggle, what examples are most efficient for modeling the strategies, and about how long the students will need for guided practice before most of them can work independently—with few, if any, notes or prompts. When interns assume responsibility for teaching the subsequent lesson, this lack of a written plan is hardly the model we want them to use.

With planning expertise so experience based, mentors may find it difficult to recognize interns' need for support. Their ease of planning reflects years of experience with the subject matter and keen knowledge of student development. An analogy for planning skills that I use with mentors is based on driving: beginning drivers consciously distinguish between the brake pedal and gas pedal. They pause momentarily to turn on the blinkers in order to not turn on the windshield wipers. Three-point turns are often six-points turns. Seasoned drivers, on the other hand, can merge through multiple lanes of traffic while talking on a hands-free device and drinking coffee during their busy morning commute. They do not think twice about the brake and gas pedals, having compressed them thousands of times. In the same way, so much of what is automatic for mentors is brand new for interns. The means that their lesson plans will look very different! A mentor's ability to articulate the rationale and thought processes behind lesson plans is imperative for fostering interns' planning skills.

Questions: At the Heart of Learning to Plan

The factor of time is one of the most prominent barriers to planning. Elementary interns in particular are faced with designing lessons for multiple subjects, each with its own set of standards, textbooks, resources, and benchmarks. We encourage interns to begin by coplanning one subject area with their mentors. By focusing on one subject, such as math, interns can concentrate on a single set of standards and probe their mentors about decisions made for one content area.

Creating lesson plans during the preinternship coursework is quite different from creating lessons that they will be teaching to "real" students. The easy component is finding the standard they must teach—most districts have pacing guides with a suggested sequence of objectives for each subject area. But knowing what students have to learn is just the first step. As they coplan with their mentor, questions to ask can include:

- How did you determine what students already know about this concept?
- How will we challenge the students who have already shown mastery of the content?
- How will we determine what students have learned from the lesson?
- How will we differentiate for the student(s) who speak a language other than English/who read below grade level/who have an IEP?

These are just some of the questions the interns should be considering as they begin to design their lessons. As the lesson plans are created, mentors should continue to think out loud about their decisions for aspects such as pacing time frames, assessment formats, print and technology resources, and key questions.

After they have observed and cotaught the subject, they are ready to start leading lessons. Despite this background with observing and coteaching, the interns are often surprised how hard it is to concentrate on teaching content while also managing behavior, engaging students, pacing appropriately, and making on-the-spot decisions regarding a myriad of situations. Their mentors made it look so easy! At this point, they should begin to consider questions such as these as they plan:

- Have I accounted for the full class period, with approximations for time frames of each component?
- How will I present directions?
- How will I determine what they know and what they have learned?

Experienced teachers know how to maintain high levels of time on task, even when lessons end earlier than expected. With academic learning time playing a key role in student success (Mulholland & Cepello, 2006), we strive to make interns aware of making every minute count. However, until they are faced with that "down time" when lessons have finished before the end of the period, they often do not recognize the value of overplanning. As noted by Lucy:

> I did a read aloud on Wednesday that went really well. The problem came when we still had about 5 minutes before we could begin the lining up process. I felt like a deer in the headlights. After a few agonizing seconds of that "Oh no, what do I do now" feeling . . . I realized I needed to always OVER plan . . . Today, I did the read aloud during the same time period. This time however, I had thought ahead. . . . I felt much better about today's lesson because I was prepared for the "what if" of extra time. From now on, I'm making sure I have at least a short something to do in case that happens again.

Similarly, interns may not consider the importance of clear directions with visual templates or models until they are faced with confused looks or are repeatedly answering the same question. A revelation occurs: It's surprisingly complicated to break down a task into simple steps extemporaneously. When teaching a social studies lesson to first-graders, Amelia noted:

> I did not make a model of the activity we were doing to show the students before they started because I thought it was something we could do together. . . . If I could go back, I would have made the model before the lesson started to show them the finished product before they started cutting and gluing on their own.

Also, there were quite a few components to the activity. After our read aloud, I explained the whole activity to the students before they went back to their desks to start. . . . I realized this was too much information and directions all at once. If I were to do this lesson again, I would explain each step one at a time so the students would not be overwhelmed with directions.

A third component of planning is measuring students' prior knowledge and outcomes. Initially, many new teachers have an egocentric view of what an effective lesson looks like: if they finish teaching without losing control of the class, they feel successful. This is usually expressed as something along the lines of, "Today was great! I got through my lessons!" However, as their experience increases, they should begin looking at the effectiveness of a lesson through the lens of student outcomes.

To determine what students learned as a result of the lesson, the interns need to know the level of students' understanding beforehand. In some content areas, this may be obtained from standardized testing from the previous year, or school system benchmark tests throughout the year. We also discuss the untapped potential of in-class diagnostic tests. Due to time constraints, these are not often used extensively; when they are, however, interns are often amazed at the impact the results can have on their planning. Jane's experience with diagnostic testing of second-graders' grammar skills was "eye-opening" for her:

Last week I gave a pre-assessment on contractions. I gave it thinking that most of my students would "ace" it and then I wouldn't have to spend as much time on contractions that week during reading. I came to find out, however, that most of my students did not know how to use contractions properly. The pre-assessment was eye-opening, and completely changed my plans for the week! It showed me the importance of not only assessing student learning, but also assessing students' prior knowledge to know where to begin teaching and what needs to be addressed.

Similarly, the assessment data obtained after a lesson has been taught provides interns with the information they need for either reteaching or continuing. Rather than determining that a lesson was successful by its mere completion, interns begin to focus on data analysis to make decisions for future instruction. As their experience continues, they can refine those decisions on a finer scale—rather than making decisions about the class as a whole, they can begin to disaggregate the data to determine outcomes such as the percent changes among various academic groups in the class. Initially, however, the recognition that assessment should drive future plans is important. After coteaching a first-grade math lesson on time, Amelia shared what she learned from giving an assessment:

Last week we gave our students the math test about telling time to the hour and the half hour. . . . We thought they had mastered this during the lesson, but the assessment showed that they were still having trouble. We decided to go back and reteach the class after the assessment, as well as include these types of problems in their morning work activities.

From these experiences, interns learn valuable lessons about pacing and preparation. They realize that those extra few minutes at the end of a lesson lead to either extended time for learning or extended time for managing off-task behavior. They recognize the importance of diagnostic assessments when trying to teach content for which their students are woefully unprepared and therefore frustrated, or when students' proficiency leads to boredom. Given that time on task has such a profound effect on student learning, it's imperative for interns to use every instructional opportunity.

PREPARING FOR FORMAL EVALUATIONS

Our interns are evaluated with both the state model for teacher evaluation (the Tennessee Educator Acceleration Model, or TEAM) and the edTPA as part of their requirements for earning their teaching licenses. They are exposed to the TEAM rubrics for planning, instruction, and environment in their preinternship courses, as we focus components of their field experience observations on indicators from these rubrics. The edTPA rubrics are presented at the beginning the internship year rather than during the preinternship to ensure that the interns have accurate information about requirements. Although the models differ in both duration and rubric components, they both require interns to demonstrate evidence of effective teaching. We have an overview of the rubrics, but they do not drive our discussion: we look first at effective teaching and second at the specific requirements of the rubrics.

In other words, we begin preparing for the evaluations by *not* focusing on the evaluations. Instead, we focus on effective teaching strategies from the start of their preinternship courses. Starting with the first week of the school year, the interns post a weekly Electronic Journal Reflection (EJR) on our web-based course site in which they respond to a prompt such as the following:

• In reflecting on one lesson you taught this week, what is one aspect you learned about your teaching (what you would definitely not do again, what you would definitely do again, what you might modify if you taught the lesson again)? On what are you basing the decision to change or not to change some aspect of the lesson?

- Depending on your school and grade level, you may have math and/or reading groups. If your classroom has ability grouping for one or more subjects, how are those groups determined? If you don't have math or reading groups, how are the learning needs of students on either end of the spectrum (low and high achievers) met?

These prompts are designed to support interns' professional development by targeting their reflections on their lesson design and lesson outcomes. This ultimately reinforces what edTPA and their state evaluations require. Schon's (1983) description of how practitioners "reflect-in-action" provides some insight regarding how teachers make decisions while they are engaged in the act of teaching. Similarly, "reflection-on-action" provides the benefit of hindsight as teachers consider what occurred and what could have occurred. The weekly EJRs provide a public (viewable by other interns in the cohort) form for reflecting on action, and the evaluation process documents both reflection-in-action and reflection-on-action through comparing how a lesson unfolds relative to the intended lesson plan and considering what changes would be made to a lesson in retrospect.

The "Dry Run" Evaluation

After six weeks in their main placement classroom, the interns move to a new school and grade level to broaden their teaching experience for the next six weeks. During this rotational placement, they have a practice evaluation that we refer to as the "dry run." For the dry run, we go through the steps they'll take during a formal evaluation. They prepare a lesson plan, are observed teaching that lesson, complete a written reflection, determine their self-scores on the associated rubrics, and participate in a conference with me or with the graduate assistant about their lesson. This promotes familiarity with the process as well as the rubrics on which they'll be evaluated.

During the observed lessons, I type a rough transcript and include timestamps about every five minutes to provide pacing information. The transcript is sent electronically to the interns right after the lessons. After the interns have read the transcript, reviewed assessment data, and reflected, they submit a written reflection on what they consider to be the areas of strength and the areas for improvement. They also complete a self-score of the indicators on the TEAM rubric for Instruction and Planning, which will be shown in greater detail later in the chapter. When we meet, we discuss four aspects:

- the intended lesson versus the implemented lesson
- self-identified strengths and weaknesses of the lesson

- assessment data from the lesson
- their self-scores from the TEAM Instruction and Planning rubrics

The Lesson Plan: Intended versus Implemented

When we meet to discuss the lesson, we begin by comparing the lesson plan to what actually occurred in the lesson. Interns can share their thought processes about how they "reflected in action" in making on-the-spot decisions during the lesson. While there are typically changes in the lessons based on behavior issues, the changes made in response to academic student cues are more frequent as their experience progresses. As we review the transcript of their lesson, we can address the "why" behind the more spontaneous actions that were not detailed in the lesson plan. For example, the intern may have shortened or lengthened a time frame for a certain portion of a lesson, run out of time to complete a final assessment, adjusted for technology that was not functioning as expected, or modified group work based on behavior. This part of the discussion focuses on what actually happened.

We also talk about the lesson from a hypothetical perspective. If you could teach this again, in what ways, if any, would you change a portion of the lesson plan based on the outcome of the lesson? These changes can be both content based and procedural based. For example, we might discuss strategies to determine students' fluency with finding common denominators prior to teaching fraction addition. Or we might brainstorm proactive steps to avoid a repeat of having a student cry for nearly five minutes about getting the red pointer instead of the pink one. Retrospective considerations can help the interns determine strategies that could be implemented in future lessons, such as using diagnostic testing to determine students' readiness for content. These considerations also help them realize that no one can accurately predict every student's reaction to a teacher's action. Until they are faced with the wailing kindergartner who does not approve of the color of the pointer she was handed, interns may never consider the color of manipulatives to be of any importance. Once they have experienced this or a similar situation, they know they need to consider proactively what they'll do when using manipulatives of varied colors, such as obtaining a set of items in the same color, or perhaps more beneficial to students in the long run, discussing appropriate reactions prior to distributing material of different colors.

Areas to Improve and Areas of Strength

Next, we discuss the interns' written reflections about what they felt went well and where they want to improve. In these reflections, interns often focus on the management aspect of the lesson as an area to improve. Amelia noted after her dry run evaluation:

I would say that my area of refinement would be behavior management. During the lesson, my students talked out without raising their hands a bit more than I would have liked . . . A few of the students also were up and moving around (going to the trash can, etc.) when they should not have been . . . I would like to have more control over their behaviors, especially when my mentor is out of the room and I am the only authority figure present.

In their preinternship courses and in their field experience, the interns have discussed or witnessed proactive management strategies, such as prefacing questions with "Raise your hand if you can tell me . . ." if that's how the teacher wants students to indicate they know an answer. However, putting this strategy into action when they are processing multiple events occurring simultaneously—thinking about the question, considering whom they should call on to answer and think about the question, seeing a student get up from her seat and wander into another area of the classroom, noting the time on the clock and realizing that there are only fifteen more minutes until it's lunchtime—is much harder when every decision still requires a concerted effort.

Similarly, Samantha noted:

The behavior was atrocious and the reasons for such inappropriate, off-task behavior could be explained on many things. To name a few, I would say . . .

1. A child's outburst where he refused to come out of his desk and then when he did, he ran out of the room.
2. The power shutting off right before I began my lesson.
3. The lack of normalcy. Typically, we do the [publisher's] video that teaches the children the concept or strategy.
4. The fact that I did not prepare my kids for the unusual shift in what we do in math.

Going back to the driving analogy, interns are consciously determining how to respond to each new situation. No course textbook ever taught them what to do when, just as they are ready to start their evaluated lesson, the power goes out and a student chooses to hide under a desk. New teachers must draw on their beliefs about teaching and their limited practical experiences to respond to situations such as these; with increased experience, they will not only recognize but also implement the proactive strategies that can be taken to create situations rather than just respond. Samantha recognized how her lack of preparing the students for a schedule change contributed to the management issues.

Along with the areas to improve, we also talk about what the interns considered to be the strengths of their lesson. Both Amelia and Samantha selected their activities/materials as the strong points of their lessons. Amelia's reflection about her choice of materials focused on both the affective and cognitive benefits of her lesson design:

> I think all of my students really enjoyed the activities we did for this lesson, especially the muffin tin activity. Not only did they enjoy it, but they also learned from it . . . I think the students liked being able to make models using tangible objects, rather than only drawing them.

The incorporation of engaging materials and limited reliance on textbook-based resources is in part a reflection of the interns' background in content-based methods courses. These courses, taken prior to and during their internship, include a strong emphasis on subject-specific pedagogy and teacher-determined resources.

Assessment Data

Next, we discuss the assessment data: What did the students learn, and how did you know what they learned? We highlight the need for direct alignment between the stated objective and the assessment. If students are expected to "identify the four stages of an insect's life cycle such as the butterfly," then the assessment needs to reflect students' ability to identify those stages. Although this sounds like a pedestrian exercise, it's actually a sticking point for many interns. That one-to-one correspondence between the objective and the assessment of the objective is essential. After we have talked about this alignment, we may discuss the expansion of data sources strategies for monitoring student progress, such as maintaining a checklist to record students' responses to questions or creating rubrics with performance criteria for longer written tasks.

Analyzing the Lesson with Evaluation Rubrics

Once we have reviewed the lesson plan, the strengths and weaknesses, and the student data, we are ready to look at the lesson through the lens of the evaluation rubrics. We have waited until this point to review the rubrics to reinforce the mantra that *effective teaching is effective teaching*. Interns need to be aware of the indicators by which they will be evaluated, but they also need to recognize that evaluation systems evolve. Tailoring their lesson to a particular rubric reduces the art of teaching to the monitoring of a checklist, rendering the evaluation process to a procedure that they must endure rather than the opportunity to reflect on the effectiveness of a lesson. Their teaching should be informed and guided by research-based strategies, not the rubric du jour.

The TEAM Instruction rubric (http://team-tn.org/evaluation/teacher-evaluation/) is a five-point scale consisting of twelve indicators. The indicators include:

- Standards and objectives (lesson objective and level of student mastery)
- Motivating students (establishment of relevancy)
- Presentation of content (lesson preview, communication strategies, modeling)
- Lesson structure and pacing (coherency, varied rates as appropriate, time on task)
- Activities and materials (resource choices)
- Questioning (cognitive levels of questions, distribution of questions, wait time)
- Academic feedback (purpose, frequency)
- Grouping students (student roles, individual accountability, effectiveness)
- Teacher content knowledge (accuracy, connection of material)
- Teacher knowledge of students (anticipated difficulties, student interests)
- Thinking (types and opportunities to exhibit)
- Problem-solving (types and opportunities to exhibit)

Although the rubric has five levels of performance, only three levels are articulated. Level 1 (Significantly Below Expectations), Level 3 (At Expectations), and Level 5 (Significantly Above Expectations) include specific details regarding performance, whereas Levels 2 and 4 do not.

Prior to our conferences, interns complete a self-score on the Instruction and Planning rubrics. I also evaluate the lessons with the rubrics, giving ranges of scores ("in the 2 to 3 range") to show what elements of the indicators were met and/or exceeded. After we've discussed the scores, we return to the self-identified areas of strength and areas for improvement, and connect those to the rubrics. Rather than just commenting on behavior in general as an area to improve, we address it in terms of the Instruction rubric. For example, perhaps the behavior issues stemmed from unclear directions for group work. This would fall under the Grouping Students indicator. Or perhaps, as in Amelia's case, there was insufficient modeling prior to having students attempt an activity independently. This would fall under the Presentation of Instructional Content indicator. What I hope to convey to the interns through their completion of self-scores and their open-ended reflections is that both processes can identify the same strengths and weaknesses—it's just that the self-scores are tied to the rubrics whereas open-ended reflections are tied to their current understanding of what constitutes effective teaching. The indicators on the rubrics just give us a placeholder and descriptor for the areas of strength and weakness rather than determine what their teaching should look like.

THE INITIAL EVALUATION FOR STATE LICENSURE

After six weeks in their rotational placement, the interns return to their main placement. This marks the thirteenth week of the school year. Upon their return, interns display a considerably higher level of confidence in their teaching abilities, which is matched by an increase in their teaching effectiveness. Returning to their main placement is similar to a homecoming; they are familiar with the school, the students, and their mentors as they have maintained either virtual or face-to-face contact during their six-week rotation.

At some point between weeks thirteen and eighteen, the interns have their first formal evaluation, which is combined with an edTPA "dry run." The interns take the lead for planning, teaching, and assessing a sequence of math lessons. One of the lessons is evaluated, and one (which can be the same) is video recorded as practice for the edTPA documentation. Initially, we simultaneously conducted a state evaluation and the actual edTPA documentation in the fall. However, we moved the schedule for edTPA to the spring semester, allowing for a trial run with video recording a lesson. The main benefit of moving to the spring was the practice with video recording and the ability for peer review of the dry run video recording during our class session in the fall. With the actual edTPA videos, we could not have peer reviews. It should be noted that the externally scored edTPA results were roughly the same whether the interns completed teaching the lesson sequence in the fall or the spring semester. More information about the edTPA implementation will be included in the next chapter.

The sequence of events for the formal TEAM evaluation for Planning and Instruction is similar to their practice version. One difference for the formal evaluation is a preconference to discuss the lesson plan. As part of our conference, the interns can provide insight regarding instructional strategy choices, grouping choices, and content presentation. We can also discuss how they determined students' readiness for the math lesson and—that typical sticking point—how they will measure student outcomes.

For her first formal evaluation, Alana's math lesson assessment included multiple opportunities for students to demonstrate their understanding of polygons. Technology-based formats as well as teacher questions were used to determine whether students showed mastery or needed reteaching. One area of assessment that we discussed in the preevaluation conference was the purpose of articulating criteria for mastery. Returning to the backwards design approach (McTighe & Thomas, 2003; Wiggins & McTighe, 2008), we discussed how teachers need to identify not only what students should be able to do at the end of the lesson but also how the students' level of mastery will be measured. There were several instances in the assessment portion of the lesson plan where Alana indicated she'd be making these determinations, but the criteria were not included. In the technology-based portion of the assessment, both the initial and revised lesson plan included the following statement:

> When students move to the "Digital Center," they will have to create four poly-
> gons on a geo-board, take a picture of the board using the Skitch App on the
> iPad, and use the app to correctly name each polygon. I will look at each of the
> pictures to assess how well my students understand what a polygon is and how
> we classify them.

During the conference, we discussed what criteria she would use to determine how well students understood the material. The revised lesson plan added the details about that aspect:

> I will consider students to have mastered the material if they create four differ-
> ent polygons and correctly identify each of them. I will consider the students
> to be struggling if they cannot create four polygons or if they incorrectly label
> any of them.

By adding this specific criterion, Alana would not have to decide during the lesson how she was going to determine mastery—students needed to be able to distinguish between a polygon and nonpolygon, and also needed to identify the polygons they created. She knew ahead of time what she expected of her students for this portion of the assessment and would be able to quickly determine who needed reteaching.

In reviewing the TEAM Planning rubric, the Assessment indicator identifies the articulation of criteria for mastery for the stated objective. However, our primary purpose in focusing on this aspect during the prelesson conference was to have her recognize this as an important attribute of any formal assessment, regardless of the fact that including this information would increase her score for this indicator. With each intern's prelesson and postlesson conference, our discussion began with a conversation about effective practices, and then related those practices to the TEAM rubric by which they were evaluated.

By the end of the fall semester, interns complete two of their five formal evaluations, complete an edTPA practice session with a self-analysis and peer analysis of a video recorded lesson, and have a better understanding of the challenges—and benefits—of effective teaching. They recognize by this point that designing effective lessons for "real" students is markedly different from lesson plans designed during the preinternship. Jane's description of this was similar to what other interns noted at the end of the fall semester:

> The most unexpected challenge of teaching is differentiating instruction! We learned so much about this during undergrad and graduate classes, but differentiating like crazy for fake lesson plans is very different than actually meeting my students' needs.

Jane continued this line of reflection about the spring semester when considering her goals for the spring:

> Next semester I hope to get very comfortable with weekly planning . . . I've always planned specific subjects or reading groups for a week at a time, but I have yet to really look at and think about every subject area for the entire week. Obviously I will continue to coplan with my mentor, but I really like to learn how to make sense of things on my own. I feel that I need to make sense of weekly planning so that I understand how it works! How much to plan? How to think about the time? What happens if everything gets finished early . . . by a few days? Or takes a few days longer than expected? I've considered these questions in specific lesson plans, but not over the course of a week.

With these experiences behind them, the interns are ready to progress to the spring semester during which they assume a greater role in leading the planning, teaching, and assessment of their students. Their experiences in the spring semester will be the focus of chapter 10.

Chapter Ten

Spring Semester: Overlaying Effective Teaching with edTPA Rubrics

The start of the fall semester is full of questions for interns: "Who are my students? Will I be able to teach alongside my mentor? How will I be treated by the school community? How will I balance the demands of my coursework, my teaching responsibilities, and my personal life?" The start of the spring semester is much different. Interns are familiar with their mentor, their students, and their school. They think back to the previous year and recall how full they thought their schedules were back then. They are still focused on coursework but are beginning to look ahead, polishing their résumés and considering the school systems to which they will apply. The end of the internship is in sight, but before they get to that point, they know that successfully completing the edTPA is one of the tasks they must accomplish.

In this chapter, we'll look at three areas associated with the spring semester. First, we'll describe how the interns progressively grow into their roles as teachers. Second, we'll look at how their action research or problem-based research review influences their teaching. Finally, we'll discuss how edTPA blends into our existing teacher preparation program.

GROWING INTO THEIR ROLES AS TEACHERS

If you picture a child in an oversized business suit, with drooping shoulders, dangling sleeves, dragging pant legs, and clown-sized shoes, that is similar to how many interns picture themselves on the first day of their internship. They may look—and feel—out of place, like trying to fit into someone else's clothes that are several sizes too big. They have minimal input at the start of the year: the management policies, the instructional strategies, and the assessment decisions are, for the most part, based on what their mentors determine.

By the start of the spring semester, however, the interns have grown into their teaching role in the classroom. They view themselves less as underlings and more as coteachers. They recognize that their teaching experience and writing requirements for coursework will exponentially increase, but they are ready for these challenges. During the spring semester, they lead more of the planning, teaching, and assessing; they complete either an action research project or a problem-based research review of the literature; and they complete the requirements for their edTPA submission. They want to assume more teaching responsibilities, even with the recognition that they will be spending an extensive amount of time designing effective lessons.

Leading, Not Soloing

With the onset of state policies altering pay scales for teachers, our department's policies related to interns' teaching responsibilities needed to reflect this new pressure of linking test scores with teacher pay. While the standardized tests scores were always an important data source for teachers and schools, the implementation of performance-based pay raises was poised to have serious consequences for the amount of direct teaching experience in which our interns could engage. A balance between providing enough opportunities for interns to gain substantial teaching experience and for the mentors to feel confident with students' preparation for standardized tests was needed.

One strategy we used for striking this balance was to replace the *solo teaching* weeks with *lead teaching* weeks during the spring semester. Seasoned mentors (and I myself, on occasion) still used the phrase *solo teaching* while adjusting to the new format. *Solo teaching* generally refers to an extended period of time during which teacher candidates "take over all classes, tangential duties and responsibilities" (Pellegrino, 2010, p. 68). Regardless of terminology, however, there was concerted effort to replace this model of having an intern independently in charge of a full week—or weeks—of instruction with little support from their mentors. *Lead teaching*, on the other hand, implies just what its name indicates—interns take the lead on planning, teaching, and assessing, but they are still under the guidance of their mentors throughout those designated weeks. Their mentors are present in the classroom and provide input as needed during lessons. In some cases, the interns and mentors continue to coteach the lessons that the intern developed, particularly when small groups are used for differentiation.

Similar to the fall semester, mentors and interns are provided with a suggested schedule for the interns' assumption of greater teaching responsibilities for the spring semester. Table 10.1 shows the calendar for the first four weeks of the spring semester. I defer the final decision about the schedule

Table 10.1 Suggested Calendar for Beginning of Spring Semester

Week	Intern/Mentor Actions
21 *(first week back in spring)*	*Intern and mentor*: Review the math unit of instruction the intern will teach as part of the edTPA requirements. edTPA math units can begin this week or during the next three weeks. Regardless, interns should be actively engaged with planning and teaching math this week.
22	*Intern*: Teach math/continue to prepare for your edTPA math unit.
	Mentor: Provide daily feedback pertaining to the math lessons that your intern is teaching. Possible areas on which to focus include Lesson Structure and Pacing or Questioning.
23	*Intern*: Begin or complete teaching your edTPA math unit. If you have already finished, begin teaching a content area unit of science or social studies, or reading if these subjects are not taught independently at your grade level. Begin planning for a lead teaching week.
	Mentor: Review plans for lead teaching week together. Review postunit assessment data together to determine the effect of instruction on student gains during the math unit.
24	*Intern*: 1) Finish teaching the edTPA math unit, if not already completed, or 2) teach a content area (social studies or science, if taught independently at your grade level, or reading) unit of instruction, or 3) lead teaching (NOTE: Mentors should still play an active role, but the intern can take the lead for planning, teaching, and assessing all lessons).
	Mentor: Debrief at the end of each day regarding student performance, behavior, and any adjustments needed for the next day's lessons.

for the extent of teaching responsibilities to the mentors and interns, as each classroom setting is unique and each intern's progress is individually determined. Demonstrating that they are on a trajectory for increasing their responsibilities matters more than the slope of the trajectory.

Viewing Themselves as Teachers

The benefits of increasing interns' responsibilities are reflected in not only their teaching expertise but also their self-confidence. As Amelia noted, her first lead week in the spring semester altered how her students viewed her. This is probably a reflection of how she viewed herself as well—when she had more responsibility, she was not just "the intern" but was the "real teacher," with all of the lessons for that week hinging on her preparation. After completing the week, she noted:

> I felt a mix of emotions all week. I was stressed while planning and even some while teaching because I was constantly worried that I would forget something important. However, it was such a good experience and I loved feeling like a "real" teacher. I think the past week really helped me with my behavior management in the classroom. At the beginning of the week, the students were a little . . . energetic. After a couple days of getting used to me teaching all day and seeing that I do have the authority to reward/punish as needed, they began to behave much better and see me as the teacher, not just the intern. It was a long, exhausting week, but I really enjoyed it and I hope my students continue to see me as a "real" teacher.

In viewing themselves more as teachers, the interns can begin to recognize that their input is valued by their mentors. Initially, interns often think that the professional development flows in one direction with their mentors—they view themselves as the only ones who are learning. However, upon reflection, they realize that they have influenced their mentor in cognitive-based or affective-based instructional domains. As Mackenzie led more of the math teaching in her first-grade classroom, she noted how her lesson structure was readily accepted by her mentor:

> At the beginning of the year, our math block was solely whole group. When I took over math, I tweaked it so it was more differentiated. We start with whole group, then those who understand the concept continue on their own, practice the concept, then move on to math centers. The struggling group, usually 4–6 students, works with me. She's told me that she's impressed with the math routine and likes that our advanced students aren't bored for half of the lesson because they're excited to move onto centers. It's so exciting to hear that someone with 30 years of teaching experience can take away something from teaching with me.

Similarly, Alana recognized that her mentor noted the time she took to interact with students, and the resulting benefits of these interactions:

> One thing I do remember [my mentor] commenting on was that I have taught her that she needs to take extra time to talk to the kids and try to connect with them. A couple of times this semester, she has told me that she feels so busy planning lessons and being the authority figure that she forgets to relax and enjoy her time with the kids. She told me that this is one of my strong suits (especially with some of our more difficult boys) and that she needs to remember that they need someone to teach them, but also someone to listen to them.

Recognizing Beliefs about the Importance of Education

As interns assume more responsibility for teaching, they begin to face a challenge they may never have encountered personally: What do you do when students—and possibly their parents—don't seem to care about how well you teach? What if they don't value education as much as you do? This can be a source of great frustration. After all of the time they are putting into their lessons, they can be demoralized when they are met with apathy.

To support interns' recognition of their own beliefs in this area, they respond to a prompt that probes their beliefs associated with the value of education. The prompt states:

> Your enrollment in this internship program shows that you have not only successfully completed an undergraduate degree but have also met the qualifications to enter an advanced degree program. Reflecting on your own educational background, what were the expectations for you as a student? Were you expected to follow a college degree path because of siblings or parents who did the same? What value did your family place on education, and how was that communicated to you? How does the value you place on education affect your interactions with students or parents who don't share those same views? Consider these questions in your reflection this week.

Depending on the school setting in which they are interning, their students may have similar or different backgrounds compared to their own upbringing. Recognizing not only the source of their own beliefs associated with the value of education but also how those beliefs are manifested in their teaching practices can help them support their students, regardless of whether those beliefs are similar or different. Samantha noted the parallels with the values of her parents and the parents of her students, which influenced her to implement teaching practices that mirrored her own experiences:

> Although I was more independent in high school and college as I completed assignments, my mother still asked frequently how I was doing. I never had to show her my grades, but I did have to assure her that I was doing my best work. The value that I place on education impacts the way I interact with my students in the way of completing assignments and being organized . . . By communicating with parents at [my school], I know they have similar opinions as my mother did in regards to education, so I know that they would want me to stay on top of their kids when it comes to being responsible.

Alana, on the other hand, noted how her beliefs were sometimes in contrast with her fifth-grade students, even though their backgrounds were similar:

> My own educational background has really affected who I am as a teacher. When I look at my kids at [this school], I see myself. I see lower-middle-class

children who are struggling to make their lives better. Because I understand where they are coming from, I try to be a role model for them and let them know how important education really is . . . One day one of my students said he did not want to be at school, and I reminded him that he was there to get a good education so he could get a good job and make a good life for himself. He told me, "Well, my mom said she never did well in school and she is fine, so my grades don't really matter." I was completely shocked . . . While I cannot change this parent's mind about education, I can have an effect on this student. Throughout the year, I will continue to encourage him to try to do well in school and remind him why school is important.

With increased experience, the interns begin to realize how their beliefs impact their practice, and their practice impacts their beliefs. Caudle and Moran (2012) found similar results working with early childhood interns. In their research, they found that interns' awareness of the "transactional nature of their beliefs and practice" occurred after gaining teaching experience (p. 46). The value the interns place on education continually inspires them to find ways to influence their students' beliefs about education. To increase their students' engagement and interest in learning, they seek ways to approach the content in a more learner-centered fashion and make the learning more relevant. Lucy succinctly described how her teaching practices reflected her desire to influence students' beliefs about the importance of education:

> For students, I take it as a personal challenge to find something that will pique their interest in hopes that they will catch the fire that learning is fun.

THEORY INTO PRACTICE: ACTION RESEARCH AND PROBLEM-BASED RESEARCH REVIEW

Before 2013/2014, all interns in our department completed an action research project as part of their graduate coursework and their master's degree requirements. This capstone experience commenced in the fall semester with the identification of a research topic, and continued in the spring with a literature review, data collection, data analysis, discussion of findings, and public presentation in a university-based conference setting. While the format of the presentations evolved over time (moving from overhead transparencies to computer-based formats), the premise was the same: by connecting theory to practice through action research, our teacher preparation model was designed to develop reflective practitioners who made data-based decisions.

As both state evaluation requirements and graduate coursework during the internship increased, the demands on the interns were intense. Then, with the implementation of edTPA, as a department we began to review the internship

requirements from all sides—our requirements for licensure, the state requirements for licensure, and our requirements for the master's degree. What
we determined was that the edTPA reflected much of what we wanted the
interns to do with action research. They were using research to design their
lessons, implementing the lessons, analyzing the data, reflecting on the effectiveness of their instruction, and using that data to make plans for subsequent
lessons. The 2012/2013 cohort, referred to as Cohort 1 in the Coda, was the
final cohort to complete an action research project.

The action research was replaced by a problem-based research review, or
PBRR. The PBRR was designed to engage interns with educational research,
but it was more limited in scope than action research. The final paper contained the following elements:

- Research topic
- Rationale
- Review of the literature
- Implications for the classroom
- Reflections on the review process

My suggestion to the interns was to connect their PBRR research topic
with the topic of their edTPA lesson sequence. For example, Kathleen's
research topic and her edTPA both focused on supporting her first-grade
students with a conceptual understanding of place value. Her research topic
stated the following:

> The development of two-digit place value understanding in the elementary
> grades serves as a prerequisite skill for ability and success in later mathematics.
> Educators must seek to understand the critical areas that should be the focus of
> place value instruction. The following review of literature will explore how to
> diagnose common error patterns and increase conceptual understanding through
> the intentional use of manipulatives and language.

The decision to connect the PBRR with the edTPA topic was purpose-
ful. Conducting a literature review develops familiarity with research-based
practices. In other words, it's crucial to distinguish between knowing what
to teach (derived from standards) and knowing how to teach it (derived from
research and experience). Additionally, the PBRR requirements for research
went above and beyond the level needed for documenting edTPA. By im-
mersing themselves in the research, the interns' instructional decisions were
more informed than if they had just determined themselves how they were
going to teach. Finally, by gaining experience with more technical writing,
they were better prepared to answer the commentary prompts on edTPA.

BLENDING THE EDTPA INTO
OUR TEACHER PREPARATION PROGRAM>

The age-old riddle of "Which came first: the chicken or the egg?" was applicable to the situation we faced when adopting the policy of having our interns complete the edTPA with blind scoring. Would edTPA then drive the methods by which I prepared interns to teach effectively, or would we continue focusing on effective teaching, which would now be evaluated according to both our state framework and the edTPA rubrics?

Supporting the Interns during the edTPA Process

Like many cohort supervisors in our teacher licensure program, I wanted the interns to view this performance-based assessment as documentation of the teaching they were already doing rather than an assessment around which we rebuilt our program. Given the dynamic nature of state and national policies related to teacher preparation, it seems impractical to reconfigure the methods by which we prepared our teachers just to meet the current set of evaluation rubrics. Instead, it made more sense to continue our focusing on effective strategies first, and looking at how those strategies were embedded in the edTPA rubrics second. So, in answering the question for teacher preparation: effective teaching continues to come first.

This is not meant to imply that we did not address any facet of the edTPA at all in our program. In some areas, we merely accentuated and extended topics we were already discussing. Other aspects were unique to the edTPA and required additional course time. Interns were provided with a suggested sequence of steps as an overview of the edTPA process. Figure 10.1 shows the bulleted list, which was modified annually based on edTPA requirements.

In class sessions, we discussed the following topics, which were pertinent to completing the edTPA:

• terminology used in the commentary prompts and rubrics
• strategies for not exceeding page limit requirements
• factors to consider when video recording

Terminology discussions are based on the issued edTPA handbooks. The glossary section of the handbooks provides interns with the technical definitions they need to accurately complete many of the commentaries. Phrases such as *central focus* are defined and explained in the handbook, thereby diminishing much of the ambiguity that arises during an initial reading of the commentary prompts.

Steps for edTPA Math Lesson Sequence

1. Distribute and collect the video permission forms

2. Review the edTPA Commentary Prompts (Planning, Instruction, Assessment)

3. Determine the math learning segment objectives from either Common Core, County standards, or TN Curriculum Framework (whatever your school is using for the standards) that you will teach in three to four lessons

4. Pre-assess the learning segment objectives.
   Note: If the pre-assessment you are using covers more than the lessons you are using for edTPA, only address the data pertaining to the objectives in the edTPA lessons in any commentary.

5. Use the TEAM lesson plan template to create daily lesson plans for the learning segment (3-4 lessons)
   a. Include criteria for evidence of mastery for each formal assessment
   b. Identify how you will address academic language (what are the key vocabulary terms students will need to know; what symbolic language do they need to know; etc)
   c. Be explicit about differentiation strategies based on IEPs and student assessment data

6. Teach the 3-4 lessons
   a. Videorecord at least one of the lessons
      i.   The videorecorded lesson should include "respectful" teacher-student interactions as well as student-student interactions
      ii. The videorecorded lesson should include a portion

Figure 10.1a   Suggested Sequence of Steps for Completing edTPA

Strategies for not exceeding page limits include removing any rationale components in lesson plans, as the rationale component is included in the written commentaries. Additionally, the interns have been working on writing either an action research paper or a problem-based literature review, so they have experience with concise technical writing. This kind of writing is differs greatly from what many were used to doing for college term papers—after many years of meeting an expectation for the minimum number of pages,

which connects learning to prior instruction as well as personal relevance

iii. If a student does not have permission to be videorecorded, seat the student out of the field of vision. The student's voice can be heard, but his/her face cannot be visible.

b. Write daily reflecting commentary in rough form

c. Save one copy of your lesson plan without the reflection and one copy of your lesson plan with the daily reflection, written after you have taught. The reflection should be based on student assessment data and indicate what you will change about the next day's lesson, if anything. The original lesson plans are what you'll submit, but the one with reflections will help you recall aspects of how the lessons unfolded.

d. Save copies of student work that includes your written feedback to them. You will be analyzing assessment data from a whole group perspective and for three focus students.

i. The three focus students will include at least one student who has an academic IEP, is gifted, ELL, or underperforming.

ii. The three should represent the "patterns of learning" of your students.

7. Post-assess the learning segment objectives. This can be with the pre-assessment you used.

8. Save all artifacts and all typed commentary for editing

Figure 10.1b   Suggested Sequence of Steps for Completing edTPA

they are now forced to fit their thoughts in a maximum number of pages. They need to be able to cite evidence and be succinct, but not to the point of writing as if they were texting a BFF.

Technology factors have to be considered when video recording, but there are other factors as well. As an example, when an intern taught a math lesson sequence that incorporated points on a coordinate plane, she wanted to make the content more contextual. To do this, she used a map of the school

and its surroundings to show the relative position of the school with different community landmarks. This lesson happened to be the one she selected
to video record for her edTPA documentation, as she anticipated a high level
of interest and engagement. When editing the video and reviewing the criteria, however, she realized that one restriction for documentation was to not
identify the school at which the lessons were conducted. She was able to use
other components of the video, but in hindsight, it would have been much less
stressful to record a lesson that did not have multiple references to the school.

Finally, even before our teacher licensure programs incorporated the
edTPA, we always focused on using basic statistics such as percent change
to analyze student test data and note patterns of achievement. Questions such
as—Are students of all academic levels being challenged and supported, or
are some groups (for example, the top 25 percent of students) not being challenged enough?—can be answered through the use of this calculation. The
review of basic statistics continued to be emphasized after the implementation of edTPA, as the percent changes provided evidence of students' growth
based on the lesson sequence.

Changes to the Program

Although I retained many of the same assignments, readings, and projects for
the internship year even after the addition of edTPA, there were also modifi-
cations made to support the interns. Specifically, I made two changes based
on the interns' feedback and the edTPA requirements. First, as mentioned in
chapter 9, I changed the implementation time frame for the edTPA lesson
sequence. Initially, the interns conducted their edTPA lesson sequence in the
fall semester because we had always video recorded a lesson for reflection
in the fall semester. When we transitioned to edTPA, I just extended this assignment to include the rest of the edTPA requirements. The spring semester
entailed the compilation of commentaries and editing of videos for a mid-
March submission deadline.

With our most recent cohort in 2013/2014, I moved the edTPA lesson sequence to the spring semester to allow for the "dry run" of planning a math
unit, video recording at least one lesson, and conducting a peer review of
the lesson during a class session in the fall. This dry run provided several
benefits. The interns gained additional experience with designing a sequence
of math lessons. They obtained feedback on aspects such as questioning and
pacing from peers. The practice of video recording also supported the interns
with the technology aspect of edTPA, such as ensuring that the audio quality
was high enough to hear students' responses. The stakes for the video were
much higher now that they were submitting it for blind scoring as part of
edTPA, so having the technology glitches worked out ahead of time allowed

the interns to focus more attention on the content of their lessons rather than equipment-related issues.

The second change based on the incorporation of edTPA pertained to the interns' professional development in the area of academic language. We often think of language as the vocabulary associated with content; however, particularly in mathematics, there is also a vast amount of symbolic language. There are also syntax elements to consider. Given the complexity of academic language, I added several resources to our coursework as reference material for the interns. We used Zacarian's *Mastering Academic Language: A Framework for Supporting Student Achievement* (2012) as our course textbook, and approached language much more deliberately than in previous years. I had often given examples to interns of academic language in terms of vocabulary. For example, a "fair" experiment in a science lesson does not mean that everyone gets the same materials to use—it refers to controlling variables. I also shared examples from my own children, such as when my daughter came home from school completely perplexed about why her fifth-grade teacher was only talking about right angles when clearly on the diagrams there were left angles too. Unbeknownst to her teacher, she spent the full lesson interpreting the term *right angle* as directional based rather than degree based, and although she was confused, like many students she would never consider raising her hand to get clarification.

In addition to the vocabulary associated with content, however, it was also important to have interns realize the symbolic language of a content area, such as signs associated with inequalities, fractions, and number sentences. Having students compare and contrast in paragraph form is different from asking them to complete a Venn diagram; they must know not only the content but also the format in which to present the differences and similarities, for example. The Zacarian (2012) book provided examples of language use from various grade levels and content areas, which supported the interns beyond just thinking of academic language for their edTPA content area.

As their opportunities for leading instruction increased, the interns commented less on management issues and more on the caliber of their instructional strategies in their reflections. In many cases, the reflections pertained to their awareness of language. When Kathleen reflected about one of her most successful lessons, she described her considerations of language in a first-grade math lesson that she led:

> I was nervous about the topic because it was the first time they've even heard the word "regroup" . . . I wanted to go really slow and pay attention to the language I was using. We spent a lot of time thinking about what the word *regroup* might even mean. I think really understanding how the word applies to what you are actually doing would have helped me a lot as a kid. I learned the procedure

of regrouping . . . but I never truly understood what I was doing. I certainly couldn't have drawn a visual for it or explain it in my own words—you just did it. When I approached this topic with my students we made a list of what we thought the word might mean and tried to apply it to real life.

Evidence of Success

Until the edTPA moved beyond the piloting stage, our teacher licensure program set its own expectations for what constituted "passing." Benchmarks were set for individual rubric scores (such as a limit on the number of 1's and 2's), and cohort supervisors were given the discretion of requiring revisions for any portion that failed to meet their expectations. In the first year of blind scoring, the eighteen members of the 2012/2013 cohort (referred to as Cohort 1 in the Coda), all of whom completed their lesson sequences in the fall semester and polished their commentaries in the spring semester, scored at or above the national field test averages on all but one of the fifteen rubrics of the Elementary Math edTPA, with an average of 46.5. In 2013 to 2014, the average for the cohort on the Elementary Math edTPA was 46.7. The Coda contains detailed information about Cohort 1's scores.

More importantly, however, the edTPA experience demonstrated to the interns that focusing solely on the rubrics during their internship year was not a requirement for passing. Rather, their attention to attributes of effective teaching supported their successful completion of the edTPA. We addressed the components that were unique to that evaluation tool, but the tool itself did not drive our approach. The lasting impression this should leave on the interns is that their first and foremost concern should be the extent to which their instructional strategies are meeting the needs of their students. Although they need to be aware of the rubrics by which they are evaluated, their focus can be—and should be—on effective teaching.

Even though we approached the edTPA as just another evaluation tool, was the experience completely stress-free? Hardly. The fear of failure was, at times, overwhelming. In her final EJR (Electronic Journal Reflection) of the semester, Samantha made an acrostic poem for TPA that exemplified how many of them felt while waiting for their scores to be returned:

Terrifying
Professional
Assessment

Alana, who wrote her final EJR after learning that she had passed, made a similar acrostic with a slightly more positive spin—"Terrifying Possible Achievement"—and added:

After I actually started working on it, I realized that although it would take a lot of time, edTPA was *possible*. After completing each step of the process I would tell myself, "That actually wasn't too horrible!" When I finished filming, I realized I had plenty of clips I could use. When I finished writing a prompt, I realized I could discuss how I was utilizing data and research to inform my instructional decisions. Although the commentaries were challenging at times, I realized my pre-internship and internship experiences had prepared me to pass. When I finally finished edTPA, I was overwhelmed by the sense of *achievement* I felt. While it may sound ridiculous, completing edTPA was one of the most challenging yet rewarding things I have ever done.

The phrase *challenging yet rewarding* also sums up how we want the interns to view teaching as a profession. The models by which they are evaluated will come and go, but the positive impact that effective teachers make on their students will last a lifetime.

Coda: The Importance of an Inquiry-Based, Workshop Approach

On a daily basis, teachers confront complex decisions that rely on many different kinds of knowledge and judgment and that can involve high-stakes outcomes for students' futures. To make good decisions, teachers must be aware of the many ways in which student learning can unfold in the context of development, learning differences, language and cultural influences, and individual temperaments, interests, and approaches to learning. In addition to foundational knowledge about these areas of learning and performance, teachers need to know how to take the steps necessary to gather additional information that will allow them to make more grounded judgments about what is going on and what strategies might be helpful. Above all, teachers need to keep what is best for the child at the center of their decision making. (Darling-Hammond & Bransford, 2005, pp. 1–2)

We believe that preparing the kinds of teachers described above is crucial, however challenging it might be during this time of "'misguided regulatory intrusions' . . . from state and federal departments of education [that] have a negative effect on teacher education programs" (Bransford, Brown, & Cocking, 1999, p. 189). Indeed, in the current policy climate, it is even *more* important that candidates take an inquiry stance into their teaching careers, considering how practices and policies work for or against equity, and working always to enhance their "students' learning and life chances for participation in and contribution to a diverse and democratic society" (Cochran-Smith & Lytle, 2009, p. 146). We don't believe this can be achieved if candidates continue to be "urged to use student-centered, constructivist, depth-versus-breadth approaches in their education courses" while they continue to "see traditional teaching approaches in use at the college level" (Bransford et al., 1999, p. 192). We believe that what is required is that they experience an inquiry-based approach themselves.

We have talked a great deal in this book about the importance of teaching for understanding—for children. This is so different than traditional teaching for recall on tests that one of the most powerful frameworks designed to support it is called *backward* design (McTighe & Thomas, 2003; Wiggins & McTighe, 2005). *Backward.* Despite its counterintuitive nature, planning and teaching for deep understanding are supported by research in the learning sciences as critical to the capacity for transfer to new situations: "transfer is affected by the degree to which people learn with understanding rather than merely memorize sets of facts or follow a fixed set of procedures" (Bransford et al., 1999, p. 43). It is imperative that our candidates themselves experience situations designed to support their learning with understanding, and thus their subsequent capacity to transfer important learning to new situations.

Optimal environments for the support of learning with understanding are simultaneously learner centered, knowledge centered, assessment centered, and community centered (Bransford et al., 1999). They provide learners opportunities for engaged participation in authentic tasks (Hickey & Zuiker, 2005; Jurow, Tracy, Hotchkiss, & Kirshner, 2012) with feedback that occurs

> continuously, but not intrusively, as a part of instruction. Effective teachers continually attempt to learn about their students' thinking and understanding. They do a great deal of on-line monitoring of both group work and individual performances, and they attempt to assess students' abilities to link their current activities to other parts of the curriculum and their lives. (Bransford et al., 1999, p. 128)

While Colleen is a literacy educator and Kristin is a science educator, we have for many years collaborated successfully in sharing students—from undergraduate initial licensure candidates through doctoral students—beginning many years ago when Colleen was supervising the interns and Kristin was teaching their preinternship course. While we come from different disciplinary backgrounds, we share a passion for inquiry-based teaching, and believe this is why students move seamlessly between us.

In the work described here, there are ever-increasing amounts of content we must bring to our candidates, and we are committed to providing opportunities for their engaged participation (Hickey & Zuiker, 2005; Jurow et al., 2012) in *applying* this content *with support*, and to that purpose we set aside time in class to allow us to respond to them as they work. In previous chapters we've described our class sessions devoted to responding to our candidates' works-in-progress, whether learning plans, preparations for TEAM or edTPA assessments, practice-based research reviews, or whatever else came along during their program. Whether we label these times as a literacy "workshop" or as a science "laboratory," the important things are

1. creating a space in which our candidates engage in genuine inquiry as they solve situated (Lave & Wenger, 1991; Wenger, 1998), real-life problems, and
2. being there to respond as needed.

We know that teacher educators are living under a microscope with high-stakes assessments driven by Race to the Top and edTPA added to what was already in place related to licensure requirements, academic degree requirements, and NCATE, CAEP, or other accreditation requirements. In this chapter we share results suggesting that our inquiry-based focus on learning for understanding did not interfere with our candidates' success on these critical measures.

HOW DID CANDIDATES RESPOND?

The results we have to share come from one cohort's TEAM (our official state teacher evaluation system) and edTPA results, and narrative reflections from the candidates in two cohorts. Because we do not ask our candidates to give informed consent to use their materials until after the school year is finished and grades and all other evaluations are completed (in order that they not feel coerced into participation), we are sharing internship-year data (TEAM and edTPA) only from the first cohort.

TEAM Results

Interns in our program are observed and evaluated formally at least three times during their internship year; these formal observations are in addition to innumerable informal visits to their classrooms by Kristin or her graduate assistant. Evaluators have the option to carry out more than three formal evaluations if needed, such as if one of the three is unacceptable. The schedule of these formal observations, and the TEAM rubrics used to assess each, are shared in table 11.1.

The array of observations are carried out by three different evaluators, using three different rubrics (some more than once), with some of the visits announced ahead of time and some unannounced. TEAM is the same system used for all teachers in Tennessee, so our interns are being evaluated according to the same criteria as in-service teachers.

Table 11.1.   Schedule of TEAM Observations and Evaluations during Internship Year

Timing	Announced or Unannounced	Evaluator	Rubric(s) of TEAM Assessed
Fall	announced	University faculty or GA supervisor	Planning Instruction
Spring	unannounced	University GA or faculty supervisor *(reverse of above)*	Environment Instruction
Spring	announced	Principal or other LEA staff	Environment

All eighteen interns in the 2012 to 2013 cohort were successful in meeting the standards of TEAM and in being recommended for licensure.

edTPA Results

Elementary candidates completing edTPA have a choice between submitting lessons in literacy or in mathematics; Kristin's interns all completed the Elementary Mathematics content area and submitted their materials to Pearson for external scoring. According to the *2013 edTPA Field Test: Summary Report* (Stanford Center for Assessment Learning and Equity, 2013), 3,669 candidates submitted complete sets of materials to Pearson, with 929 of those being Elementary Mathematics submissions. The "common architecture" (Stanford Center for Assessment Learning and Equity, 2013) of edTPA allows comparisons across content areas with all submissions being evaluated according to five Planning rubrics, five Instruction rubrics, and five Assessment rubrics, as described below.

Task 1 Planning

Planning for Instruction and Assessment is measured according to the following rubrics that lead to scores #1 through #5 of a candidate's submission.

1. Planning for Content Understandings
2. Supporting Students' Learning Needs
3. Using Knowledge of Students to Inform Planning
4. Identifying and Supporting Language Demands
5. Planning Assessment to Monitor Student Learning (Stanford Center for Assessment Learning and Equity, 2013, p. 11)

Table 11.2 includes results on Task 1 Planning for our Cohort 1, for Elementary Mathematics nationwide, and for all content areas in the field test.

Table 11.2.   2013 edTPA Scores for Task 1: Planning

Subgroup	Score 1	Score 2	Score 3	Score 4	Score 5	Total
Cohort 1 mean Elementary Mathematics						
n = 18	3.35	3.29	3.65	3.00	3.24	16.53
edTPA field test mean Elem Mathematics						
n = 929	3.29	3.17	3.19	2.99	3.08	15.72
σ	*0.67*	*0.79*	*0.72*	*0.65*	*0.74*	
edTPA field test mean All Content Areas						
n = 3669	3.15	2.98	3.02	2.95	2.96	15.06
σ	*0.75*	*0.87*	*0.75*	*0.71*	*0.84*	*3.15*

Task 2 Instruction

Instructing and Engaging Students in Learning is assessed according to the following rubrics that lead to scores #6 through #10 of a candidate's submission.

1. Demonstrating a Positive and Engaging Learning Environment
2. Engaging Students in Learning
3. Deepening Learning during Instruction
4. Subject-Specific Pedagogy
5. Analyzing Teaching Effectiveness (Stanford Center for Assessment Learning and Equity, 2013, p. 11)

Shown in table 11.3 are results on Task 2 Instruction for our Cohort 1, for Elementary Mathematics nationwide, and for all content areas in the field test.

Task 3 Assessment

Assessing Student Learning is assessed according to the following rubrics that lead to scores #11 through #15 of a candidate's submission.

1. Analyzing Student Learning
2. Providing Feedback to Guide Learning
3. Supporting Students' Use of Feedback
4. Evidence of Language Use to Support Content Learning
5. Using Assessment to Inform Instruction (Stanford Center for Assessment Learning and Equity, 2013, p. 11)

Table 11.3. 2013 edTPA Scores for Task 2: Instruction

Subgroup	Score 6	Score 7	Score 8	Score 9	Score 10	Total
Cohort 1 mean Elementary Mathematics						
n = 18	3.24	3.00	3.00	3.06	3.12	15.41
edTPA field test mean Elem Mathematics						
n = 929	3.15	3.05	2.97	3.02	2.83	15.02
σ	0.51	0.61	0.67	0.61	0.71	
edTPA field test mean All Content Areas						
n = 3669	3.12	2.90	2.87	2.78	2.68	14.35
σ	0.58	0.69	0.75	0.84	0.75	2.77

Table 11.4 includes results on Task 3 Assessment for our Cohort 1, for Elementary Mathematics nationwide, and for all content areas in the field test. Of note are problems with scoring rubric #13 that required student use of written feedback from candidates last year; those who have taught kindergarten, first grade, or other students with limited literacy skills will be able to imagine how challenging it would be to meet this criterion with authenticity—if at all—in some settings. Similar to the 2012/2013 guidelines, candidates may this year submit audio or video artifacts of the feedback they give to students. However, none of the candidates selected the options of a video or audio clip as it was difficult to document through these methods due to concerns about the quality of the audio. If evaluators could not understand the students due

Table 11.4. 2013 edTPA Scores for Task 3: Assessment

Subgroup	Score 11	Score 12	Score 13	Score 14	Score 15	Total
Cohort 1 mean Elementary Mathematics						
n = 18	3.00	3.18	2.35	2.82	3.29	14.65
edTPA field test mean Elem Mathematics						
n = 929	2.96	2.99	2.62	2.64	2.92	14.13
σ	0.79	0.86	0.80	0.68	0.86	
edTPA field test mean All Content Areas						
n = 3669	2.83	2.90	2.38	2.52	2.73	13.36
σ	0.86	0.88	0.82	0.74	0.91	3.39

to low volume or accent, there would be no useful evidence of feedback. According to the 2013/2014 guidelines, candidates can now provide a transcription of up to two pages from the video or audio clip, making a video or audio clip a more viable option.

Additional changes in Task 3 include the increase in the number of permitted pages of the assessment and directions/prompts. The previous limit was two pages; in the 2013/2014 guidelines, the page limit is now five. To demonstrate students' understanding and use of the targeted academic language function, candidates had been restricted to one or two sources (the video submitted for Task 2 and/or student work samples). According to the 2013/2014 guidelines, candidates can now include up to three sources, as an additional video clip (up to five minutes) of one or more students using language within the learning segment can be included.

It is interesting to note that the documentation for the assessment task has had the most revisions of the three. While restrictions on file lengths and artifact choices remain a challenge of edTPA documentation for Task 3, the increased number of options for candidates is a positive step toward the accurate representation of how candidates determined their students' level of mastery as related to conceptual understanding, procedural fluency, and problem-solving skills.

edTPA Total Score and Cutoff

The Stanford Center for Assessment, Learning and Equity (SCALE) offers the following advice for interpretation of edTPA scores:

- Level 1 represents the low end of the scoring spectrum, representing the knowledge and skills of a struggling candidate who is not yet ready to teach.
- Level 2 represents the knowledge and skills of a candidate who is possibly ready to teach.
- Level 3 represents the knowledge and skills of a candidate who is ready to teach.
- Level 4 represents a candidate with a solid foundation of knowledge and skills for a beginning teacher.
- Level 5 represents the advanced skills and abilities of a candidate very well qualified and ready to teach. (Stanford Center for Assessment Learning and Equity, 2013, p. 12)

While these individual scores are reported, SCALE reports that scorers evaluate a candidate's entire submission, rather than rely on independent scorers of discrete, isolated tasks. This approach allows the scorer to effec-

Table 11.5.   2013 edTPA Total Scores

Subgroup	Total Score
Cohort 1 mean Elementary Mathematics	
n = 18	46.59
edTPA field test mean Elem Mathematics	
n = 929	44.87
edTPA field test mean All Content Areas	
n = 3669	42.76
σ	*8.17*

tively review the entirety of a candidate's teaching evidence. Total scores for our Cohort 1, for Elementary Mathematics nationwide, and for all content areas in the field test are displayed in table 11.5.

An edTPA standard-setting procedure led to a recommendation that a maximum total score of no more than 42 be set as a cutoff when edTPA is being used for such, and included pass-rate data for a band of scores between 37 and 42, representing those scores within one standard error of measurement of the maximum recommended cut score (Stanford Center for Assessment Learning and Equity, 2013). Our state has not yet set a passing score, but at UT we set a cutoff of 37. All of our candidates scored 37 (mean of 46.59) or higher, and were able to use their edTPA scores to replace the Principles of Learning and Teaching Praxis exam otherwise required in Tennessee for initial licensure.

Candidates' Reflections

In this section we share short reflections from our candidates at various times, to complement those of Hannah and Jessica in this volume. Like many candidates, Cathie recognized that the in-class work time supported her success at a complex task: *When it comes to the creation of the learning plan, I was so thankful that we were given so much time and help on it. . . . otherwise, I feel like things would have been super overwhelming for me.* Elsie also reflected on how much less dangerous the high-stakes assessments seemed from the vantage point of a supported learning environment:

> I appreciate more than anything in this experience, how prepared we are for the crazy year that is ahead of us because of this class. The way that you incorporated the TEAM and edTPA stuff together, while treating us like humans who have the capacity to actually enjoy their work. And enjoy it I did! I would have failed miserably if you had told us to just memorize some rubric or study what we are supposed to do during edTPA, but I feel really prepared because I have a better understanding of how to do those things well because I actually enjoy them!

Maggie reflected on the safety of the environment that supported her as a
risk taker, and how she wants to accomplish that in her own teaching:

> I want there to be a culture of acceptance within my room, where every learner
> feels safe and comfortable to ask questions and to learn. . . . To conclude, I
> want to reiterate that I have greatly appreciated a class environment where I
> can convey my own interpretations of things. And not only is this allowed, but
> my perceptions are also valued and acknowledged rather than criticized. I am
> grateful for the way you modeled constructive criticism against misconceptions.
> Additionally, you made our learning environment open and safe, which is why
> I have placed such an emphasis on similar conventions as mentioned in the
> paragraph above.

Maggie's reflection that she felt safe to speak, and to make mistakes, on
her learning journey emphasizes how important it is that we continue to find
ways to overcome those "grading policies in college classes that can under-
cut collaboration" (Bransford et al., 1999, p. 189) if we wish our candidates
to take the risks necessary to understand deeply, rather than to pass a test.
Sarah's reflection is further evidence of the power of such an environment, as
she describes how it inspired her to use its support to work on subject matter
she was afraid of:

> I decided that previous to this semester the subject that seemed scariest to me to
> teach was reading . . . I chose to do language arts because I knew it was what I
> needed the most help teaching. I know you love reading and love to teach teach-
> ers how to teach so I chose this area because I knew I would have good support
> when I needed help.

How refreshing that she chose subject matter she was nervous about so that
she could get better, instead of choosing an area in which she was confident to
make an A, which might have been her choice in a more traditional academic
setting. And how fortunate for her children.

Finally, here is a reflection from Kathleen written during her internship
year, in the midst of being evaluated by both the TEAM and edTPA rubrics:

> While preparing for evaluations, when I do have moments of self-doubt after
> concerning myself with the rubrics for far too long, I repeat the questions that
> Colleen taught us to ask—Who are my students? What do I want them to learn?
> How will I know when they've learned it? Once I can answer these questions, I
> am able to regain focus and approach each challenge with reclaimed confidence.
> This is also true in regards to preparing for edTPA. . . . Though I believe that
> both the TEAM and edTPA rubrics include valuable ideals that are integral to
> increasing the standards of success in schools today, as a new teacher the pres-
> sure of checking off each item under every indicator is daunting. To keep us

grounded while working on edTPA, at each class meeting Dr. Rearden reminds us that this assessment is simply an opportunity to showcase the good teaching we are already doing. With such a reminder, we are able to place our focus where it should be—on the students, not the rubrics.

DISCUSSION

We believe that the evidence we have available of different types (narrative as well as quantitative), from different tools (edTPA, TEAM), from different evaluators (connected to UT, connected to LEA's, and Pearson), and used for candidates at different stages of their careers (preinternship, internship, in-service), converges to demonstrate that by focusing on teaching for deep understanding, rather than for a specific rubric or evaluation scheme, we are not doing our candidates a disservice even when those schemes and rubrics are high-stakes phenomena in their professional lives. This is critically important at a time when our profession is in such flux that there is every reason to believe that the systems in place during a candidate's preservice preparation will not be there once she begins teaching . . . or three to five years down the road. We are, we hope, preparing teachers for twenty- or twenty-five- or thirty-year careers, not simply for success on this year's rubric; it is more relevant than ever that we are able to prepare teachers who can design and carry out learning plans aimed at deep understanding, which can then be overlaid by rubrics for edTPA, state teacher evaluation, or even Common Core State Standards. There is a need to move beyond rubrics as course or syllabus topics, and to prepare candidates for success in a constantly changing professional life. Toward this end, we have focused our efforts on helping our candidates

1. plan and teach for deep understanding,
2. document the important things they are doing in their planning and teaching, and
3. articulate those things according to the terminology of the particular scheme or rubric by which they are being assessed.

We believe that the essential questions supporting planning and teaching for deep understanding are endurable, and that the final step of "translating" those into the specific rubric language required is transferable to whatever system in which they may find themselves, including TEAM or edTPA themselves, which are not static. We cannot overstate the importance of an inquiry-based, workshop approach in our work with teachers toward these goals, and end by returning to it one more time.

Lorri Shepard (2011) has described the writing workshop

> as both assessment tool and prompt for productive interactions, whereby children develop an understanding of themselves as authors who receive feedback as a natural part of improving. (p. 27)

We view our in-class work sessions as spaces for our candidates to develop an understanding of themselves as professionals who receive feedback as a natural part of improving—and not only as part of unnatural, high-stress and high-stakes formal assessments. Just as writing teachers focus first on students' meaning, and then on how to use the mechanics of language to communicate that meaning (Calkins, 1994; Graves, 1983; Graves & Hansen, 1983; Hansen, 2001; Harwayne, 2001), we work with our candidates first to focus on good teaching, and then to translate that for the various audiences to whom they are accountable.

Bibliography

Adams, L. (2011). Learning a new skill is easier said than done. GordonTraining.com.

American Statistical Association. (2014). ASA statement on using value-added models for educational assessment. Alexandria, VA: American Statistical Association.

Baker, B. D., Oluwole, J. O., & Green, P. C. (2013). The legal consequences of mandating high stakes decisions based on low quality information: Teacher evaluation in the Race-to-the-Top era. *Education Policy Analysis Archives, 21*(5), 1–65.

Bartholomae, D. (1985). Inventing the university. In M. Rose (Ed.), *When a writer can't write: Studies in writer's block and other composing process problems* (pp. 134–65). New York: Guildford.

Bergeron, B. S. (2008). Enacting a culturally responsive curriculum in a novice teacher's classroom: Encountering disequilibrium. *Urban Education, 43*(4), 4–28.

Bransford, J., Brown, A. L., & Cocking, R. R. (1999). *How people learn: Brain, mind, experience, and school.* Washington, DC: National Academy Press.

Calkins, L. M. (1994). *The art of teaching writing.* Portsmouth, NH: Heinemann.

CAST. (2011). Universal design for learning guidelines version 2.0. Wakefield, MA.

Caudle, L., & Moran, M. (2012). Changes in understandings of three teachers' beliefs and practice across time: Moving from teacher preparation to in-service teaching. *Journal of Early Childhood Teacher Education, 33*(1), 38–53.

Chandler-Olcott, K., Kliewer, C., & Petersen, A. (2010). *Presuming competence in inclusive literacy pedagogy: Theorizing connections between multiple literacies and disability studies perspectives.* Paper presented at the Literacy Research Association, Fort Worth, TX.

Cochran-Smith, M., & Lytle, S. L. (2009). *Inquiry as stance.* New York: Teachers College Press.

Curtis, R., & Wiener, R. (2012). Means to an end: A guide to developing teacher evaluation systems that support growth and development. Washington, DC: Education & Society Program.

Darling-Hammond, L. (2006a). Assessing teacher education. *Journal of Teacher Education, 57*(2), 120–38. doi: 10.1177/0022487105283796

Darling-Hammond, L. (2006b). *Powerful teacher education.* San Francisco: Jossey-Bass.

Darling-Hammond, L. (2013). *Getting teacher evaluation right: What really matters for effectiveness and improvement.* New York: Teachers College Press.

Darling-Hammond, L., Amrein-Beardsley, A., Haertel, E. H., & Rothstein, J. (2011). *Getting teacher evaluation right: A background paper for policy makers.* Paper presented at the Capitol Hill Research Briefing, Washington, DC.

Darling-Hammond, L., & Bransford, J. (2005). *Preparing teachers for a changing world.* San Francisco: Jossey-Bass.

Ehlert, M., Koedel, C., Parsons, E., & Podgursky, M. (2012). Selecting growth measures for school and teacher evaluations. Washington, DC: National Center for Analysis of Longitudinal Data in Education Research.

Eisner, E. W. (2002). *The arts and the creation of mind.* New Haven: Yale University Press.

Fisher, D., & Frey, N. (2007). *Checking for understanding: Formative assessment techniques for your classroom.* Portsmouth, NH: Heinemann.

Fisher, D., & Frey, N. (2009). Feed up, back, forward. *Educational Leadership, 67*(3), 20–25.

Frey, N., & Fisher, D. (2010). Identifying instructional moves during guided learning. *Reading Teacher, 64*(2), 84–95.

Gately, S. E. (2005). Two are better than one. *Principal Leadership, 5*(9), 36–41.

Gilrane, C. P. (2014). Shifting identity in teacher development. In C. O'Mahony, A. Buchanan, M. O'Rourke, & B. Higgs (Eds.), *Threshold concepts: From personal practice to communities of practice* (pp. 138–42). Cork, Ireland: National Academy for the Integration of Research, Teaching and Learning.

Glazerman, S., Goldhaber, D., Loeb, S., Raudenbush, S., Staiger, D. O., & Whitehurst, G. J. (2012). Passing muster: Evaluating teacher evaluation systems (p. 36). Washington, DC: Brown Center on Educational Policy.

Goe, L., Biggers, K., & Croft, A. (2012). Linking teacher evaluation to professional development: Focusing on improving teaching and learning. Washington, DC: National Comprehensive Center for Teacher Quality.

Goe, L., Holdheide, L., & Miller, T. (2011). A practical guide to designing comprehensive teacher evaluation systems. Washington, DC.

Goodman, Y. M. (1985). Kidwatching. In A. Jaggar & M. T. Smith-Burke (Eds.), *Observing the language learner* (pp. 9–18). Newark, DE: International Reading Association.

Goodman, Y. M. (2011). Sixty years of language arts education: Looking back in order to look forward. *English Journal, 101*(1), 17–25.

Graves, D. H. (1983). *Writing: Teachers and children at work.* Portsmouth, NH: Heinemann.

Graves, D. H. (1985). All children can write. *Learning Disabilities Focus, 1*(1), 36–43.

Graves, D. H., & Hansen, J. (1983). The author's chair. *Language Arts, 60*(2176–183).

Hansen, J. (1983). Authors respond to authors. *Language Arts, 60*(8), 970–76.

Hansen, J. (2001). *When writers read* (2nd ed.). Portsmouth, NH: Heinemann.

Harwayne, S. (2001). *Writing through childhood: Rethinking process and product.* Portsmouth, NH: Heinemann.

Hickey, D. T., & Zuiker, S. J. (2005). Engaged participation: A sociocultural model of motivation with implications for educational assessment. *Educational Assessment, 10*(3), 277–305. doi: 10.1207/s15326977ea1003_7

Hill, D., Hansen, D., & Stumbo, C. (2011). Policy considerations for states participating in the Teacher Performance Assessment Consortium (TPAC). Washington, DC.

Jurow, A. S., Tracy, R., Hotchkiss, J. S., & Kirshner, B. (2012). Designing for the future: How the learning sciences can inform the trajectories of preservice teachers. *Journal of Teacher Education, 63*(2), 147–60. doi: 10.1177/0022487111428454

Kamens, M. W. (2007). Learning about co-teaching: A collaborative student teaching experience for preservice teachers. *Teacher Education and Special Education, 30*(3), 12.

Lanier, J. E., & Little, J. W. (1986). Research on teacher education. In M. C. Wittrock (Ed.), *Handbook of research on teaching* (pp. 527–69). New York: Macmillan.

Lave, J., & Wenger, E. (1991). *Situated learning.* New York: Cambridge University Press.

Levy, S. (1996). *Starting from scratch: One classroom builds its own curriculum.* Portsmouth, NH: Heinemann.

Levy, S. (2000). Building a culture where high quality counts. In A. L. Costa & B. Kallick (Eds.), *Assessing and reporting on the habits of mind* (pp. 84–105). Alexandria, VA: Association for Supervision and Curriculum Development.

Margolis, J. (2009). Start with the passion that fuels a teacher's soul. *Journal of Staff Development, 30*(1), 80.

Mathis, W. (2012). Research-based options for education policymaking: Teacher evaluation. Boulder, CO: National Education Policy Center.

McCarthey, S. J. (2008). The impact of No Child Left Behind on teachers' writing instruction. *Written Communication, 25*(4), 462–505. doi: 10.1177/0741088308322554

McGuinn, P. (2012). The state of teacher evaluation reform: State education agency capacity and implementation of new teacher-evaluation systems. Washington, DC: Center for American Progress.

McTighe, J., & Thomas, R. S. (2003). Backward design for forward action. *Educational Leadership, 60*(5), 52.

McTighe, J., & Wiggins, G. (2004). *Understanding by design professional development workbook.* Alexandria, VA: ASCD.

Mead, S., Rotherham, A., & Brown, R. (2012). The hangover: Thinking about the unintended consequences of the nation's teacher evaluation binge. *Teacher Quality 2.0.* Washington, DC: American Enterprise Institute for Public Policy Research.

Merseth, K. K., Sommer, J., & Dickstein, S. (2008). Bridging worlds: Changes in personal and professional identities of pre-service urban teachers. *Teacher Education Quarterly, 35*(3), 89–108. doi: 10.2307/23478983

Miller, F. Y., & Coffey, W. (2009). *Winning basketball for girls* (4th ed.). New York: Chelsea House.

Mulholland, R., & Cepello, M. (2006). What teacher candidates need to know about academic learning time. *International Journal of Special Education, 21*(2), 63–73.

Newmann, F. M., Smith, B., Allensworth, E., & Bryk, A. S. (2001). Instructional program coherence: What it is and why it should guide school improvement policy. *Educational Evaluation and Policy Analysis, 23*(4), 297–321.

Paris, S. G., & Winograd, P. (2003). The role of self-regulated learning in contextual teaching: Principles and practices for teacher preparation. In K. R. Howey (Ed.), *U.S. Department of Education project preparing teachers to use contextual teaching and learning strategies to improve student success in and beyond school*. ERIC.

Pellegrino, A. M. (2010). Pre-service teachers and classroom authority. *American Secondary Education, 38*(3), 62–78.

Perelman, L. (2008). Information illiteracy and mass market writing assessments. *College Composition and Communication, 60*(1), 128–41.

Pugach, M. C., & Winn, J. A. (2011). Research on co-teaching and teaming: An untapped resource for induction. *Journal of Special Education Leadership, 24*(1), 36–41.

Richards, H. V., Brown, A. F., & Forde, T. B. (2007). Addressing diversity in schools: Culturally responsive pedagogy. *Teaching Exceptional Children, 39*(3), 64–68.

Roth, W.-M., & Tobin, K. (2004). Coteaching: from praxis to theory. *Teachers and Teaching, 10*(2), 161–79. doi: 10.1080/0954025032000188017

Schon, D. A. (1983). *The reflective practitioner: How professionals think in action*. New York: Basic Books.

Shakman, K., Riordan, J., Sánchez, M. T., DeMeo Cook, K., Fournier, R., & Brett, J. (2012). An examination of performance-based teacher evaluation systems in five states (Issues and Answers Report, REL 2012-No. 129). Washington, DC.

Shannon, P. (1989). *Broken promises*. New York: Bergin & Garvey.

Shannon, P. (1990). *The struggle to continue: Progressive reading education in the United States*. Portsmouth, NH: Heinemann.

Shepard, L. A. (2011). Assessing with integrity in the face of high-stakes testing. In P. J. Dunston & L. B. Gambrell (Eds.), *60th yearbook of the literacy research association* (pp. 18–32). Oak Creek, WI: Literacy Research Association.

Solis, M., Vaughn, S., Swanson, E., & McCulley, L. (2012). Collaborative models of instruction: The empirical foundations of inclusion and co-teaching. *Psychology in the Schools, 49*(5), 498–510. doi: 10.1002/pits.21606

Stanford Center for Assessment Learning and Equity. (2013). 2013 edTPA field test: Summary report. Stanford, CA: Leland Stanford Junior University.

Stivers, J. (2008). 20 ways to strengthen your coteaching relationship. *Intervention in School and Clinic, 44*(2), 121–25.

Taylor, M. M. (2008). Changing the culture of "test prep": Reclaiming writing workshop. *Language Arts Journal of Michigan, 23*(2), 23–34.

University of Tennessee Office of Field-Based Experiences. (2013). *Elementary Education 351: Handbook for elementary field experience*. University of Tennessee, Knoxville. Knoxville, TN.

Urzua, A., & Vasquez, C. (2008). Reflection and professional identity in teachers' future-oriented discourse. *Teaching and Teacher Education, 24*(7), 1935–46.

Wei, R. C., Darling-Hammond, L., Andree, A., Richardson, N., & Orphanos, S. (2009). *Professional learning in the learning profession: A status report on teacher*

development in the United States and abroad. Dallas, TX: National Staff Development Council.

Wenger, E. (1998). *Communities of practice: Learning, meaning, and identity.* New
York: Cambridge University Press.

Wiggins, G., & McTighe, J. (2005). *Understanding by design* (2nd ed.). Upper Saddle
River, NJ: Prentice-Hall.

Wiggins, G., & McTighe, J. (2008). Put understanding first. *Educational Leadership,
65*(8), 36–41.

Wilson, S. M., Rozelle, J. J., & Mikeska, J. N. (2011). Cacophony or embarrassment
of riches: Building a system of support for quality teaching. *Journal of Teacher
Education, 62*(4), 383–94. doi: 10.1177/0022487111409416

Wiseman, D. L. (2012). The intersection of policy, reform, and teacher education.
Journal of Teacher Education, 63(2), 87–91. doi: 10.1177/0022487111429128

Wittgenstein, L. (1953). *Philosophical investigations.* Oxford, UK: Blackwell.

Wong, H. K., & Wong, R. T. (1998). *The first days of school: How to be an effective
teacher.* Mountain View, CA: Harry K. Wong Publications.

Zacarian, D. (2012). *Mastering academic language.* Thousand Oaks, CA: Corwin
Press.

Index

academic language, 135–36
action research projects, 129
activities: in dry run evaluation, 118–19; interviewing mentor teachers about, 96–98, *97*; in planning, 70–71; for special education, 79–80 *See also* lesson plans
American Educational Research Association (AERA), xi
American Enterprise Institute for Public Policy Research, on VAM policy implementation, xii–xiii
ASA Statement on Using Value-Added Models for Educational Assessment (American Statistical Association), xii
assessments, 45–56; authentic, vs. tests, 55–56; beyond worksheets and tests, 54–55; in course organization, 19, 21; data from, in dry run evaluation, 119; in edTPA, 142–44, *143*; evaluating and critiquing current practice, 55–56; formative, of candidates, 46–47, 52–53; intern responsibility for, 108–10; interviewing mentor teachers about, 96–98, *97*; knowledge of students in, 77–80; in lesson planning, 53–54, 114–15, 119,

121–22; of lesson plans, in dry run evaluation, 119–21; observing strategies for, 100, *101*; in optimal environment, 139; and perfectionism, 56; performance assessments, 50–52; preferred by teacher candidates, 30–31; pressure from, 100; reflections on, 79–80; in special education, 79–80; as stand-alone topic, 50–53; statistics as, 134; student experience in designing, 56; understanding in, 45, 50; in W.H.E.R.E.T.O. strategy, 82 *See also* rubrics
assigned seating, 88–89
assignments, preferred by teacher candidates, 30–31
authenticity, in course design, 11–12

backward planning: candidate learning about, 63–64; and content standards, 41; graphic organizers for, 41; in teaching for understanding, 139; in Understanding by Design (UbD) framework, 41
behavior management: in action, 118; observing, 95, *96*
beliefs, about importance of education, 128–29

cell phone etiquette, 90
child development, in instruction, 24
children's literature, selecting, 57–59
classroom: in internship, 103–5;
    observation of environments in, *94,*
    94–95, *96*; in preinternship seminar,
    88–89; preparing, 104; spectrum of
    environments in, 91–92
classroom management: in candidates'
    needs, 28–30; expectations during
    internship, 110; observation of, *94,*
    94–95, *96, 98*–100
classroom visits, viewing on tape,
    15–18, *16*
clothing, in professionalism, 90
coherence, in course design, 11–12
collaboration, in learning plan
    development, 21. *See also* group
    work
colleagues, teacher candidates as, 11,
    49–50
community, in optimal environment,
    139
conferences: addressing diversity in,
    31–32; in candidate assessments,
    47–50; in course organization,
    21–23; final, 23; grading in,
    49; preevaluation, 121–22
confidence, during internship, 126–27
content areas: academic language
    for, 135–36; candidate advice for
    teaching, 39–40, *40*; and curriculum
    standards, 37–44; integrating,
    14–18, *16*; as stand-alone topic,
    38–40, *40*; vs. student needs,
    37–44; supports for thinking about,
    38–41; symbolic language for,
    135; and understanding, 43
content standards, and backward
    planning, 41
coplanning, of lesson plans, 112
coteaching, as personnel resource,
    59–62, 65–66
course design, for teacher
    education: assessments in, 19,
21; authenticity in, 11–12; coherence
    in, 11–12; conferences in,
    21–23; content knowledge
    in, 37; diversity addressed
    in, 31–35; diversity in,
    36; feedback on, 8–9; grading
    for, 48–50; implementation of,
    12–23; learning objectives in,
    19; learning plans in, 12–13,
    19–23; models of effective teaching
    in, 14–18; organization of, 4–6, *5,*
    12–13; planning, 6–12; redesigning,
    xiv–xv, 4–6; resources in,
    19; structures and candidates' needs,
    28–30; students in, 13–14; syllabus
    in, 36
credibility, during internship, 105–7
culture, within schools, 92–93, *93*
curriculum standards: and backward
    planning, 41; and content,
    37–44; depth vs. coverage in,
    44; student understanding of, 42

Dear Colleen letters, 11, 25–27
decision making: in formative
    assessments, 47; about instructional
    materials, 57–59, 64–65; about
    instructional strategies, 59–62; about
    personnel resources, 65–66
desks, arrangement of, 88–89
diagnostic testing, for understanding,
    114
directions, in lesson plans, 113–14
diversity: addressing in conferences,
    31–32; addressing in course,
    31–35; in course organization, 36; in
    practice, 122–23; readings on, 32–35,
    33, 34; sensitivity to, 35–36; as
    stand-alone topic, 32–35, *33*
dry run evaluation, 116–21, 134–
    35; activities in, 118–19; assessment
    data in, 119; for edTPA, 121, 134–
    35; improvements in, 117–18; lesson
    plan assessment in, 119–21; for
    lesson plans, 134–36; materials

in, 118–19; resources in, 118–19; strengths in, 118–19; TEAM in, 120–21

due process, VAMs as violation of, xiii

economic diversity, addressing, 34, *34*

edTPA: action research projects and, 129–30; assessments in, 142–44, *143*; cutoff score for, 145; dry run for, 121, 134–35; four essential questions and, 9–11, *10*; instruction rubric in, 142, *143*; during internship, 71; lesson planning in, 141, *142*; modification to program and, 134–36; preparing for, 115–21, 145–47; problem-based research review and, 130; reflections in, 116; reflections on, 145–47; results on, 141–45, *142, 143, 145*; rubrics of, 6, 115, 141–45; scheduling, 121; scoring, 136–37, 144–45, *145*; stress related to, 136–37, 146–47; success on, 136–37; supporting interns during, 131–34, *132–33*; in teacher licensure, xiv; teaching for, 75; terminology in, 131, 135–36; Understanding by Design (UbD) framework and, 83

education, beliefs about importance of, 128–29

Electronic Journal Reflection (EJR), 115–16

emails, before internship, 89–90

environment: behavioral, 95, *96*; decisions about, 63; differences among, 92–93; for edTPA preparation, 145–47; for field experience, 91–92, *94*, 94–95, *96*; for internship, 103–5; for optimal learning, 139; for preinternship seminar, 88–89; using, 72–73. *See also* classroom

Equip strategy, 81

erosion unit, teaching, 72–73

evidence of learning. *See* assessments

experience, lesson plans based on, 110–12

exploration, in teaching science, 72–73

feedback: on course design, 8–9; formative assessments as, 52

field experience: assessment strategies in, 100, *101*; classrooms in, 91–92, *94*, 94–95, *96*; first impressions in, 89–90; instructional strategies in, 98–100, *99*; outcomes of, 101–2; planning process in, 95–98, *97*; during preinternship seminar, 90–100; professionalism in, 89–90; school culture in, 92–93, *93 See also* internship

The First Days of School (Wong and Wong), 88

first impressions, 89–90

first-year teaching, reflections on, 71–74

Fisher, Doug, 52

formal assessments. *See* edTPA; Tennessee Educator Acceleration Model (TEAM)

formative assessments: of candidates, 46–47; as stand-alone topic, 52–53

four essential questions: in course organization, 19; in Dear Colleen letters, 25–27; defining, 6–8; fine-tuning, 8–9; in learning plan development, 20; reflections on, 69–70; rubrics and, 9–11, *10*; in teacher education, 6–12

frameworks: for integrating content areas, 15–18, *16*; Understanding by Design (UbD), 41, 76–83

Frey, Nancy, 52

goals. *See* learning objectives

Goodman, Yetta, 24

grading: and colleagueship, 49–50; for Spring Block, 48–50

graphic organizers: for backward planning, 41; for viewing classroom visits, 15–18

Graves, Donald, 11
group work: formative assessments
    of, 46–47; monitoring during,
    98–99; preferences about,
    30–31; reasons for using, 62

Hansen, Jane, 11
higher-order levels of thinking,
    classroom example of, 15–18, *16*
history content, teaching, 79–80
Hook strategy, 81

improvements, in evaluation dry run,
    117–18
inner-city students, teaching, 71, 7
    2–73
inquiry-based learning: importance of,
    138–40; for math, 73–74; for science,
    72–73
instruction: child development in, 24; in
    edTPA, 142, *143*
instructional materials, selecting, 57–59,
    64–65
instructional strategies: observation of,
    98–100, *99*; selecting, 59–62
International Reading Association, 24
internship: action research projects in,
    129–30; beliefs about education in,
    128–29; classroom environment in,
    103–5; confidence during,
    126–27; credibility during,
    105–7; formal evaluation during,
    121–23; lesson plans during,
    110–12; observation during, 109–
    10; presence established during,
    105–7; problem-based research
    review in, 130; reflections on, 70–71,
    79–80; responsibilities during,
    108–10, *111,* 124–29, *126*; success
    during, *108–9*; suggested calendar
    for, *111, 126*; support for edTPA
    during, 131–34, *132–33*; workspace
    during, 105. *See also* field experience
interviews, of mentor teachers, 95–98,
    97

kidwatching: by teacher candidates,
    31–35; of teacher candidates,
    25–31; term used as, 24
knowledge: in learning, 7; in optimal
    environment, 139; and skills, 37–38

language: academic, 135–36; symbolic,
    135
lead teaching, vs. solo teaching, 125–26
learners: and Dear Colleen letters,
    25–27; in optimal environment,
    139; strategies and structures for,
    28–30; teacher candidates as, 28–30
learning: assessments of,
    45; classroom examples of, 15–18,
    16; and curriculum standards,
    37–44; knowledge in, 7; optimal
    environment for, 139; setting goals
    for, 78–79; tailoring, 82; in teacher
    education, 7; vs. understanding, 51
learning objectives: assessment data
    and, 119; in course organization,
    19; interviewing mentor teachers
    about, 96–98, *97*; students in setting,
    77–80
learning plans: assessments for,
    53–54; collaboration in, 21; in
    course organization, 12–13,
    19–23; differentiation enacted in,
    31–32, 122–23; observing in field
    experience, 95–98, *97*; organizing,
    82; rubrics in, 22; self-evaluation
    of, 20–21; stages in developing,
    20–21; teacher evaluation
    systems and, 71; in teaching,
    7; timing of resource decisions in,
    65; W.H.E.R.E.T.O. strategy for,
    80–82 *See also* backward planning
lesson plans: activities in,
    70–71; assessments in, 114–15,
    119, 121–22; coplanning of,
    112; directions in, 113–14; dry
    run for, 134–36; for edTPA, 141,
    142; evaluation rubrics for, 119–
    21; formal evaluation of,

121–23; improving, 117–18; intended vs. implemented, 117; during internship, 110–15; material selection in, 57–59; problem-based research review connected to, 130; questions in planning, 112–15; reflections on, 115–16; strengths of, 118–19; student outcomes in, 114; time in, 113 *See also* learning plans

Levy, Steven, 15–18, *16*

literacy content area, backward planning for, 41

The Lorax (Seuss), 70

management. *See* behavior management; classroom management

manipulatives, student reactions to, 117

Mastering Academic Language (Zacarian), 135

materials: in dry run evaluation, 118–19; instructional, selecting, 57–59, 64–65; for summative assessment, 48; in W.H.E.R.E.T.O. strategy, 81

math content, teaching, 73–74

meaning, student construction of, 73, 74

mentor teachers: behavior management strategies of, 95; considerations in matching, 103–4; expectations of, 110; lesson planning by, 110–12; performance-based pay and, 125; planning processes of, 95–98, *97*; professional development of, 127; as support for interns, *106–7, 107 See also* field experience

models of effective teaching, in course schedule, 14–18

National Academy of Education, xi

opening session, for preinternship seminar, 89

organizational styles, in internship placement, 104–5

Organize strategy, 82

out-of-context learning, vs. understanding, 51

page limitations, in edTPA, 132–33, 144

parents, beliefs about education, 128–29

pay, performance-based, and interns, 125

perfectionism, and assessment, 56

performance assessments, 50–52

personnel resources, selecting, 59–62, 65–66

planning: intern responsibility for, 108–10; skills development in, 110–15; in teaching, 7; for understanding, 43–44, 69–70. *See also* learning plans; lesson plans

policy: in inquiry-based education, 138; speed of implementation, 138

pre-assessments, 114

preinternship seminar: classroom design for, 88–89; opening session of, 89; preparation for field experience in, 89–90. *See also* field experience

presence, establishing during internship, 105–7

preservice teachers. *See* teacher candidates

presumed competence, 11–12

problem-based research review, 130

professionalism: cell phone etiquette in, 90; clothing and, 90; first impressions and, 89–90

pullout services, 60–62

puppets, in history unit, 79–80

quality control, in self-grading, 49

questions, in lesson planning, 112–15

Race to the Top Program, responses to, xi

readings: on diversity, 32–35, *33, 34*; on formative assessments, 52–53; on material selection, 57–59; on performance assessments, 50–52; preferences about, 30

reflections: on classroom "visits,"
     15–18, *16*; on edTPA, 145–47; on
     field experience, 101–2; on first-year
     teaching, 71–74; Hannah, 69–75; on
     internship, 70–71; Jessica, 76–83; on
     lesson plans, 115–16, 117; in self-
     grading, 49; in teacher evaluation
     preparation, 115–16
resources: candidate learning about,
     64–65; in course organization,
     19; in dry run evaluation, 118–
     19; environment as, 63; instructional
     materials, 57–59; instructional
     strategies, 59–62; personnel
     resources, 59–62, 65–66; sequencing
     of, 65; space as, 63; time as, 63, 65
Rethink and Revise strategy, 81–82
rubrics: of edTPA, 6, 115, 141–45; four
     essential questions and, 9–11, *10*; for
     learning plans, 22; for lesson plan
     evaluation, 119–21; self-scoring,
     120–21; teaching for, 69, 75,
     147; of TEAM, 6, 120–21 *See also*
     assessments

SCALE (Stanford Center for
     Assessment, Learning and Equity),
     144
school culture, observation of, 92–93,
     93
schools, differences between, 92–93
science content, teaching, 72–73
Seuss, Dr. (pseudonym), *The Lorax,* 70
skills: developing for planning, 110–
     15; and knowledge, 37–38
Smith, Renée, 15
solo teaching, vs. lead teaching,
     125–26
sources, in edTPA, 144
space. *See* classroom; environment
special education: coteaching in,
     59–60; reflections on teaching,
     76–83
Spring Block. *See* course design, for
     teacher education

stand-alone topics: assessments as,
     50–53; content areas as, 38–40,
     40; diversity as, 32–35, *33*
standards. *See* content standards;
     curriculum standards
Stanford Center for Assessment,
     Learning and Equity (SCALE), 144
station teaching, 60, *60*
statistics, as assessment data, 134
stereotypes, and diversity, 36
strategies: for assessments, 100,
     101; for behavior management,
     95; in candidates' needs,
     28–29; instructional, 59–62,
     98–100, *99*; for teaching, in teacher
     evaluation preparation, 115–
     16; W.H.E.R.E.T.O., 80–82
strengths, in evaluation dry run,
     118–19
students: academic language and,
     135; achievement data, within
     TEAM, xiv; in assessing learning,
     77–80; beliefs about education,
     128–29; connecting to content,
     42; curriculum standards
     understood by, 42; and Dear
     Colleen letters, 26–27; in goal
     setting, 77–80; identifying, 6, 19,
     24–36; importance of knowing,
     35–36; influence of teachers on,
     89; needs of, vs. content areas,
     37–44; in setting learning goals,
     78–79; in special education,
     77; unexpected reactions of, 117. *See
     also* teacher candidates
success, during internship, *108–9*
summative assessments: of candidates,
     47–50; materials for, 48
syllabus, in course organization, 36
symbolic language, 135

Tailor strategy, 82
teacher(s): authority in grading,
     48–49; confidence as, 126–27;
     and Dear Colleen letters,

25–27; influence of, 89; interns as, 124–29 *See also* mentor teachers

teacher candidates: advice for teaching content areas, 39–40, *40*; assessments of, 46–50; assessments preferred by, 30–31; assignments preferred by, 30–31; backward planning in curriculum of, 63–64; cares of, 27–28; class structures needed by, 28–30; as colleagues, 11, 49–50; in course organization, 13–14; course structures needed by, 28–30; familiarity with teaching models, 14–15; formative assessments of, 46–47; help needed by, 28–30; introducing in class, 89; as kidwatchers, 31–35; kidwatching and, 25–31; as learners, 28–30; responses needed by, 29–30; self-grading by, 48–50; summative assessments of, 47–50; in teacher evaluation systems, xiii–xv *See also* field experience; internship

teacher education: edTPA and, 131–34, *132–33*; four essential questions in, 6–12; inquiry-based learning in, 138–40; learning in, 7; redesigning, xiv–xv; supportiveness in, 145–47; teacher evaluation systems and, xiii–xv; tools used in, 7; understanding in, 139, 147; at University at Tennessee, Knoxville, 3–4, *4 See also* course design; field experience; internship; preinternship seminar

teacher evaluation systems: current state of, xii; dry runs for, 116–21; lack of coherence in, xi–xii; learning plans and, 71; teacher candidates in, xiii–xv; teacher education and, xiii–xv. *See also* edTPA; Tennessee Educator Acceleration Model (TEAM)

Teacher Performance Assessment Consortium (TPAC), in teacher candidate evaluation, xiv

teacher role, classroom example of, 15–18, *16*

teacher talk, in formative assessments, 52–53

teaching: confidence in, 126–27; intern responsibility for, 108–10, *111,* 124–29, *126*; lead vs. solo, 125–26; models for, 14–18; planning in, 7; strategies for, in teacher evaluation preparation, 115–16. *See also* learning; understanding

TEAM. *See* Tennessee Educator Acceleration Model (TEAM)

technology, in edTPA, 133–34

Tennessee, changes to teacher evaluation systems in, xiii–xiv

Tennessee Academic Vocabulary guide, 39

Tennessee Educator Acceleration Model (TEAM): in dry run evaluation, 120–21; four essential questions and, 9–11, *10*; initial evaluation, 121–23; during internship, 71; in learning plan development, 21; preparing for, 115–21; in reorganizing course, 5–6; results on, 140–41, *141*; rubrics of, 6, 120–21; stress related to, 146–47; teaching for, 75; use of, xiii–xiv

Tennessee Value-Added Assessment System (TVAAS), within TEAM, xiv

terminology, in edTPA, 131, 135–36

tests: assessments beyond, 54–55; vs. authentic assessment, 55–56; pressure from, 100

textbook, teaching from, 74

time: decisions about, 63, 65; in lesson planning, 113

tools, in teacher education, 7

TPAC (Teacher Performance Assessment Consortium), in teacher candidate evaluation, xiv

transcriptions, in edTPA, 144
TVAAS (Tennessee Value-Added
    Assessment System), within TEAM,
    xiv

UbD (Understanding by Design)
    framework: backward planning in,
    41; in special education, 76–83
understanding: in assessments, 45,
    50; content areas and, 43; defining,
    77; diagnostic testing for, 114; vs.
    learning, 51; planning for, 43–44,
    69–70; self-evaluation of, 82; in
    teacher education, 139, 147;
    teaching contexts and, 76–80
Understanding by Design (UbD)
    framework: backward planning
    in, 41; in special education,
    76–83

*Understanding by Design Professional
    Development Workbook* (McTighe
    and Wiggins), 20, 80
universal design principles, 11–12
University at Tennessee, Knoxville,
    elementary education program at,
    3–4, *4*

value-added models
    (VAMs): disagreement over,
    xii; limitations of, xii; speed of
    implementation, xii; as violation of
    due process, xiii
video recording, in edTPA, 133–34,
    143–44

W.H.E.R.E.T.O. strategy, 80–82
word problems, in teaching math, 74
worksheets, assessments beyond, 54–55

About the Authors

Colleen P. Gilrane is a faculty member in the Theory and Practice in Teacher Education Department at the University of Tennessee, Knoxville. She works with preservice and in-service teachers as well as advanced graduate students in literacy and in elementary education, and serves as chair of the university's Institutional Review Board. Her teaching and research interests focus on working *with* teachers to create communities in which all learners have access to literacy that is rich, powerful, and joyful.

Kristin T. Rearden is a clinical associate professor at the University of Tennessee, where she has focused on preservice teacher preparation and elementary science education for over fifteen years. She received the University of Tennessee Alumni Association's Outstanding Teacher Award in 2010 and was the Tennessee Science Teacher Association's Science Educator of the Year for Higher Education in 2012.

Hannah Louderback graduated from the University of Tennessee with a BS in Psychology and an MS in Elementary Education. During her graduate studies, Hannah completed her internship in a second-grade classroom and did research on the use of technology by students to self-assess their reading expression. After completing her degrees, Hannah was hired to teach fourth grade at a multicultural, Title I school in east Tennessee. This teaching experience enabled her to learn how to teach in a cooperative, one-to-one technology- and arts-integrated environment. After teaching fourth grade, Hannah was hired by the University of Tennessee at the Early Learning Center for Research and Practice. She is the lead kindergarten teacher, while also conducting research and mentoring undergraduate teacher candidates.

About the Authors

Jessica Covington has completed a baccalaureate and master's degree at the University of Tennessee, Knoxville. She is licensed to teach Modified and Comprehensive Special Education for grades K–12 and Elementary Education for grades K–6. In her internship year, she gained experience teaching in a Comprehensive Development Classroom for grades K–5, a fourth-grade class, and a high school resource class teaching English and world history. While completing her internship, she researched technology-based writing intervention for students with intellectual disabilities. She has been hired to teach in a Comprehensive Development Classroom-Activity Based and is looking forward to helping her students develop the skills necessary to achieve their goals.